P9-CFJ-929

Careers in Focus

ARCHAEOLOGY

Ferguson
An imprint of Infobase Publishing

Ferguson
An imprint of Infobase Publishing
132 West 31st Street
New York NY 10001

Library of Congress Cataloging-in-Publication Data

Careers in focus. Archaeology.
    p. cm. — (Careers in focus)
    Includes bibiliographical references and index.
    ISBN-13: 978-0-8160-8022-9 (hardcover : alk. paper)
    ISBN-10: 0-8160-8022-4 (hardcover : alk. paper) 1. Archaeology—Vocational guidance.
    CC107.C37 2010
    930.1023—dc22   20100224349

Ferguson books are available at special discounts when purchased in bulk quantities for businesses, associations, institutions, or sales promotions. Please call our Special Sales Department in New York at (212) 967-8800 or (800) 322-8755.

You can find Ferguson on the World Wide Web at
http://www.infobasepublishing.com

Text design by David Strelecky
Composition by Mary Susan Ryan-Flynn
Cover printed by Yurchak Printing, Landisville, PA
Book printed and bound by Yurchak Printing, Landisville, PA
Date printed: December, 2011
Printed in the United States of America

This book is printed on acid-free paper.

All links and Web addresses were checked and verified to be correct at the time of publication. Because of the dynamic nature of the Web, some addresses and links may have changed since publication and may no longer be valid.

Table of Contents

Introduction

Archaeology is concerned with the study and comparison of people in all parts of the world, their physical characteristics, customs, languages, traditions, material possessions, and social and religious beliefs and practices. Archaeologists study the physical evidence of human culture, examining such items as tools, burial sites, buildings, religious icons, pottery, and clothing. At most universities, archaeology is considered a branch of anthropology. Anthropology is a broad social science that studies human origins and our physical, social, and cultural development and behavior.

Careers in Focus: Archaeology describes a variety of careers in archaeology and anthropology—at colleges and universities; at historical societies and museums; with local, state, and federal agencies; at cultural resources management companies; at newspapers and magazines; in law offices; and with a variety of other employers. There are jobs for people who want to work behind a desk, teach students in classrooms, work in a laboratory, or get their hands dirty at an archaeological dig. Opportunities are available for 9-to-5 types, as well as globe trekkers who want to participate in digs anywhere from Montana to Madagascar. Archaeological fieldwork is conducted in countless settings—in boiling deserts, on wind-swept mountains, in caves, deep underwater, in bustling cities, in the coldest reaches of the Arctic, in tropical rainforests, and in almost any other imaginable place.

Archaeology careers are as diverse in their earnings and educational requirements as they are in their nature. Earnings range from minimum wage for entry-level field technicians to $150,000 or more for museum curators. A few careers—such as laboratory testing technicians and administrative support workers—require little formal education, but are excellent starting points for a career in the industry. A few positions only require a bachelor's degree for entry, but most require master's degrees and doctorates. The career of cultural resources lawyer requires a law degree.

The U.S. Department of Labor (DOL) predicts that employment for archaeologists and anthropologists will increase by 28 percent through 2018. This growth rate is much faster than the average for all careers. The DOL predicts that the majority of job growth for archaeologists will occur in the management, scientific, and technical consulting services industry. Most archaeological work in the United States today is done by cultural resource management firms to assess, excavate, and study archaeological sites that will be destroyed by new construction and development. Employment at colleges and universities will be weaker since there is considerable competition for jobs in these settings.

Some of the articles in *Careers in Focus: Archaeology* appear in Ferguson's *Encyclopedia of Careers and Vocational Guidance*, but have been updated and revised with the latest information from the U.S. Department of Labor, professional organizations, and other sources. Additionally, many have been written especially for this book. These include Cultural Resources Law Enforcement Officers, Cultural Resources Lawyers, Cultural Resources Management Archaeologists and Managers, Environmental Archaeologists, Ethnoarchaeologists, Field Technicians and Supervisors, Forensic Anthropologists and Archaeologists, Government Archaeologists, Private Sector Archaeologists, and Underwater Archaeologists.

The following paragraphs detail the sections and features that appear in the book.

The **Quick Facts** section provides a brief summary of the career, including recommended school subjects, personal skills, work environment, minimum educational requirements, salary ranges, certification or licensing requirements, and employment outlook. This section also provides acronyms and identification numbers for the following government classification indexes: the Dictionary of Occupational Titles (DOT), the Guide for Occupational Exploration (GOE), the National Occupational Classification (NOC) Index, and the Occupational Information Network (O*NET)-Standard Occupational Classification System (SOC) index. The DOT, GOE, and O*NET-SOC indexes have been created by the U.S. government; the NOC index is Canada's career classification system. Readers can use the identification numbers listed in the Quick Facts section to access further information about a career. Print editions of the DOT (*Dictionary of Occupational Titles*. Indianapolis, Ind.: JIST Works, 1991) and GOE (*Guide for Occupational Exploration*. Indianapolis, Ind.: JIST Works, 2001) are available at libraries. Electronic versions of the NOC (http://www23.hrdc-drhc.gc.ca) and O*NET-SOC (http://online.onetcenter.org) are available on the Internet. When no DOT, GOE, NOC, or O*NET-SOC numbers are listed, this means that the U.S. Department of Labor or Human Resources and Skills Development Canada have not created a numerical designation for this career. In this instance, you will see the acronym "N/A," or not available.

The **Overview** section is a brief introductory description of the duties and responsibilities involved in this career. Oftentimes, a career may have a variety of job titles. When this is the case, alternative career titles are presented. Employment statistics are also provided, when available. The **History** section describes the history of the particular job as it relates to the overall development of its industry or field. The **Job** describes the primary and secondary duties of the job. **Requirements** discusses high school and postsecondary education and training requirements, any certification or licensing that is necessary, and other personal requirements for success in the job. **Exploring** offers suggestions on how to gain experience in or knowledge of the particular job before making a firm educational and financial commitment. The focus is on what can be done while still in high school (or in the early years of college) to gain a better understanding of the job. The **Employers** section gives an overview of typical places of employment for the job. **Starting Out** discusses the best ways to land that first job, be it through the college career services office, newspaper ads, Internet employment sites, or personal contact. The **Advancement** section describes what kind of career path to expect from the job and how to get there. **Earnings** lists salary ranges and describes the typical fringe benefits. The **Work Environment** section describes the typical surroundings and conditions of employment—whether indoors or outdoors, noisy or quiet, social or independent. Also discussed are typical hours worked, any seasonal fluctuations, and the stresses and strains of the job. The **Outlook** section summarizes the job in terms of the general economy and industry projections. For the most part, Outlook information is obtained from the U.S. Bureau of Labor Statistics and is supplemented by information gathered from professional associations. Job growth terms follow those used in the *Occupational Outlook Handbook*. Growth described as "much faster than the average" means an increase of 21 percent or more. Growth described as "faster than the average" means an increase of 14 to 20 percent. Growth described as "about as fast as the average" means an increase of 7 to 13 percent. Growth described as "more slowly than the average" means an increase of 3 to 6 percent. "Little or no change" means a decrease of 2 percent to an increase of 2 percent. "Decline" means a decrease of 3 percent or more. Each article ends with **For More Information,** which lists organizations that provide information on training, education, internships, scholarships, and job placement.

Careers in Focus: Archaeology also includes photos, informative sidebars, and interviews with professionals in the field.

Anthropologists

QUICK FACTS

School Subjects
Geography
History

Personal Skills
Communication/ideas
Helping/teaching

Work Environment
Indoors and outdoors
One location with some
  travel

Minimum Education Level
Doctorate degree

Salary Range
$31,530 to $53,460 to
  $119,070+

Certification or Licensing
None available

Outlook
Much faster than the average

DOT
054

GOE
02.04.01

NOC
4169

O*NET-SOC
19-3091.00, 19-3091.01,
  25-1061.00

OVERVIEW

Anthropologists study the origin and evolution of humans from a scientific point of view, focusing on the ways of life, physical characteristics, languages, values, customs, and social patterns of people in various parts of the world. There are approximately 5,800 anthropologists and archaeologists in the United States.

HISTORY

Herodotus, a Greek historian, is generally considered the first anthropologist, writing in the early 400s B.C. about the people of the Persian Empire. His writings formed a foundation for centuries of studies to follow, as historians and other scholars researched the development of cultures and civilizations. The rise of imperialism paved the way for modern anthropology as Europeans took over foreign lands and were exposed to new cultures. In the early 19th century, amateur anthropologists formed their own societies. By the end of the 19th century, anthropologists began lecturing at colleges and universities.

Franz Boas, through his teachings and research, helped to promote anthropology as a serious science in the 1920s. His students included Margaret Mead and Ruth Benedict, who later established their own anthropology departments. Mead conducted fieldwork, most notably among the Samoan people, that proved ground-breaking as well as controversial; for her research, she relied more on her interaction with individual groups of people than on statistics. Approaches and explanations expanded throughout the 20th century. Today, anthropologists specialize in diverse areas, focusing on geographic areas and on such subjects as education, feminism, politics, and film and photography.

THE JOB

Anthropology is concerned with the study and comparison of people in all parts of the world, their physical characteristics, customs, languages, traditions, material possessions, and social and religious beliefs and practices. Anthropologists constitute the smallest group of social scientists, yet they cover the widest range of subject matter.

Anthropological data may be applied to solving problems in human relations in fields such as industrial relations, race and ethnic relations, social work, political administration, education, public health, and programs involving transcultural or foreign relations. Anthropology can be broken down into subsets: cultural anthropology, linguistic anthropology, and physical or biological anthropology.

Cultural anthropology, the area in which the greatest number of anthropologists specialize, deals with human behavior and studies aspects of both extinct and current societies, including religion, language, politics, social structure and traditions, mythology, art, and intellectual life. *Sociocultural anthropologists,* also called *ethnologists,* classify and compare cultures according to general laws of historical, cultural, and social development. To do this effectively, they often work with smaller, perhaps less diverse societies. For example, a sociocultural anthropologist might decide to study Romani (or Gypsies) of Eastern Europe, interviewing and observing Gypsies in Warsaw, Prague, and Bucharest. Or, a sociocultural anthropologist could choose to study Appalachian families of Tennessee and, in addition to library research, would talk to people in Appalachia to learn about family structure, traditions, morals, and values. *Urban anthropologists* are specialized sociocultural anthropologists who study the behavior and customs of people who live in cities.

Linguistic anthropologists study the role of language in a culture and how it changes over time. They study its structure and how it relates to the development of a culture.

Physical anthropologists and *biological anthropologists,* are concerned primarily with the biology of human groups. They study the differences between the members of past and present human societies and are particularly interested in the geographical distribution of human physical characteristics. They apply their intensive training in human anatomy to the study of human evolution and establish differences between races and groups of people. Physical anthropologists can apply their training to forensics or genetics, among other fields. Their work on the effect of heredity and environment on cultural attitudes toward health and nutrition enables *medical anthropologists* to help develop urban health programs.

One of the most significant contributions of physical anthropologists comes from their research on nonhuman primates. Knowledge about the social organization, dietary habits, and reproductive behaviors of chimpanzees, gorillas, baboons, and others helps explain a great deal about human behavior, motivation, and origins. People working in primate studies are increasingly interested in conservation issues because the places where primates live are threatened by development and the overharvesting of forest products. The work done by Jane Goodall is a good example of this type of anthropology.

Forensic anthropology is a branch of physical anthropology. *Forensic anthropologists* examine and identify bones and skeletal

Books to Read

Barley, Nigel. *The Innocent Anthropologist: Notes from a Mud Hut.* Long Grove, Ill.: Waveland Press, 2000.

Burns, Karen Ramey. *The Forensic Anthropology Training Manual.* 2d ed. Upper Saddle River, N.J.: Prentice Hall, 2006.

Camenson, Blythe. *Great Jobs for Anthropology Majors.* 2d ed. New York: McGraw-Hill, 2004.

Duranti, Alessandro. (ed.) *Linguistic Anthropology: A Reader.* 2d ed. Hoboken, N.J.: Wiley-Blackwell, 2009.

Haviland, William A., Harald E. L. Prins, Dana Walrath, and Bunny McBride. *Cultural Anthropology: The Human Challenge.* 12th ed. Florence, Ky.: Wadsworth Publishing, 2008.

Jurmain, Robert, Lynn Kilgore, Wenda Trevathan, and Russell L. Ciochon. *Introduction to Physical Anthropology.* 12th ed. Florence, Ky.: Wadsworth Publishing, 2009.

Miller, Barbara D. *Anthropology.* 2d ed. Columbus, Ohio: Allyn & Bacon, 2008.

Miller, Barbara D. *Cultural Anthropology.* 5th ed. Upper Saddle River, N.J.: Prentice Hall, 2008.

Smith, Cameron M., and Evan T. Davies. *Anthropology For Dummies.* Hoboken, N.J.: For Dummies, 2008.

Stanford, Craig, John S. Allen, and Susan C. Anton. *Biological Anthropology: The Natural History of Humankind.* 2d ed. Upper Saddle River, N.J.: Prentice Hall, 2008.

An anthropologist conducts field interviews. *(Michael Doolittle, The Image Works)*

remains for the purposes of homicide, scientific, archaeological, or judicial investigations.

REQUIREMENTS

High School

Follow your high school's college prep program to be prepared for undergraduate and graduate programs in anthropology. You should study English composition and literature to develop your writing and interpretation skills. Foreign language skills will also help you in later research and language study. Take classes in computers and classes in sketching, simple surveying, and photography to prepare for some of the demands of fieldwork. Mathematics and science courses can help you develop the skills you'll need in analyzing information and statistics.

Postsecondary Training

You should be prepared for a long training period beyond high school. You will first need to earn a bachelor's degree, and then go on to earn advanced degrees. More than 350 colleges and universities offer a bachelor's degree in anthropology. Before beginning graduate work, you will study such basic courses as psychology, sociology, history, geography, mathematics, logic, English composition, and literature, as well as modern and ancient languages. The final two years of the undergraduate program will provide an opportunity for specialization not only in anthropology but in some specific phase of the discipline.

More anthropologists are finding jobs with only master's degrees, but most of the better positions in anthropology will require a doctorate, which entails about four to six years of work beyond the bachelor's degree. You'll need a doctorate in order to join the faculty of college and university anthropology programs. The American Association of Physical Anthropologists offers a list of graduate programs in physical anthropology at its Web site, http://www.physanth.org/career/departmental-graduate-programs-in-physical-anthropology. A list of colleges and universities that offer degrees in applied anthropology is available at the Society for Applied Anthropology's Web site, http://www.sfaa.net/sfaaorgs.html.

Students planning to become physical anthropologists should concentrate on the biological sciences. A wide range of interdisciplinary study in languages, history, and the social sciences, as well as the humanities, is particularly important in cultural anthropology, including the areas of linguistics and ethnology. Independent field study also is done in these areas.

In starting graduate training, you should select an institution that has a good program in the area in which you hope to specialize. This is important, not only because the training should be of a high quality, but also because most graduates in anthropology will receive their first jobs through their graduate universities.

Assistantships and temporary positions may be available to holders of bachelor's or master's degrees, but are usually available only to those working toward a doctorate.

Other Requirements

You should be able to work as part of a team, as well as conduct research entirely on your own. Because much of your career will involve study and research, you should have great curiosity and a desire for knowledge. Successful anthropologists also have excellent communication skills and a passion and dedication to their work. They must also have an open mind and not have any prejudice or bias against other cultures. This respect for other cultures is extremely important, as you'll be interacting closely with people with diverse backgrounds.

EXPLORING

Anthropology may be explored in a number of ways. For example, Boy Scout and Girl Scout troops participate in camping expeditions for exploration purposes. Local amateur anthropological societies may have weekly or monthly meetings and guest speakers, study developments in the field, and engage in exploration on the local level. You may begin to learn about other cultures on your own by attending local cultural festivals, music and dance performances, and cultural celebrations and religious ceremonies that are open to the public.

Trips to museums also will introduce you to the world of anthropology. Both high school and college students may work in museums on a part-time basis during the school year or during summer vacations. The Earthwatch Institute offers student expedition opportunities to a range of locations such as India, Greece, Guatemala, and England. For descriptions of programs and recent projects, see http://www.earthwatch.org.

EMPLOYERS

The American Anthropological Association (AAA) reports that it has more than 10,000 members. Traditionally, most anthropologists have worked as professors for colleges, universities, and community colleges, or as curators for museums. But these numbers are changing. The AAA estimates that while about 70 percent of its professional members work in academia, about 30 percent work in such diverse areas as social service programs, health organizations, city planning departments, and marketing departments of corporations. Some also work as consultants.

STARTING OUT

The most promising way to gain entry into these occupations is through graduate school. Graduates in anthropology might be approached prior to graduation by prospective employers. Often, professors will provide you with introductions as well as recommendations. You may have an opportunity to work as a research assistant or a teaching fellow while in graduate school, and frequently this experience is of tremendous help in qualifying for a job in another institution.

You should also be involved in internships to gain experience. These internship opportunities may be available through your graduate program, or you may have to seek them out yourself. Many organizations can benefit from the help of an anthropology student; health centers, government agencies, and environmental groups all conduct research.

The American Anthropological Association offers links to organizations that offer internships, as well as a career center, at its Web site, http://www.aaanet.org. Additionally, the Society for Applied Anthropology provides job listings at its Web site, http://www.sfaa. net/sfaajobs.html.

ADVANCEMENT

Because of the relatively small size of this field, advancement is not likely to be fast, and the opportunities for advancement may be somewhat limited. Most people beginning their teaching careers in colleges or universities will start as instructors and eventually advance to assistant professor, associate professor, and possibly full professor. Researchers on the college level have an opportunity to head research areas and to gain recognition among colleagues as an expert in many areas of study.

Anthropologists employed in museums also have an opportunity to advance within the institution in terms of raises in salary or increases in responsibility and job prominence. Those anthropologists working outside academia and museums will be promoted according to the standards of the individual companies and organizations for which they work.

EARNINGS

According to the U.S. Department of Labor, college and university anthropology professors earned salaries that ranged from less than $41,270 to $119,070 or more in 2009, depending on the type of institution. The median salary for these professors was $69,520. Those who worked at colleges and universities earned mean annual salaries of $76,080, and those employed by junior colleges earned $73,150. In its 2008–09 salary survey, the American Association of University Professors (AAUP) reported that the average yearly income for all full-time faculty was $79,439. It also reported that professors earned the following average salaries by rank: full professors, $108,749; associate professors, $76,147; assistant professors, $63,827; instructors, $45,977; and lecturers, $52,436. Many professors try to increase their earnings by completing research, publishing in their field, or teaching additional courses. As faculty members, anthropologists benefit from standard academic vacation, sick leave, and retirement plans.

The U.S. Department of Labor reports that the median annual salary for anthropologists and archeologists was $53,460 in 2009. Salaries ranged from less than $31,530 to $87,890 or more. Salaries in urban areas are somewhat higher. Benefits include vacation and sick time, health, and sometimes dental, insurance, and pension or 401(k) plans.

WORK ENVIRONMENT

The majority of anthropologists are employed by colleges and universities and, as such, have good working conditions, although field work may require extensive travel and difficult living conditions. Educational facilities are normally clean, well lighted, and ventilated.

Anthropologists work about 40 hours a week, and the hours may be irregular. Physical strength and stamina is necessary for fieldwork of all types. Those working on excavations, for instance, may work during most of the daylight hours and spend the evening planning the next day's activities. Those engaged in teaching may spend many hours in laboratory research or in preparing lessons to be taught. The work is interesting, however, and those employed in the field are usually highly motivated and unconcerned about long, irregular hours or primitive living conditions.

OUTLOOK

The U.S. Department of Labor predicts that employment for anthropologists will grow much faster than the average for all occupations through 2018—with most job growth occurring in the scientific, management, and technical consulting industry. Despite this prediction, there will be strong competition for jobs in this field. Most new jobs arising in the near future will be nonteaching positions in consulting firms, research institutes, corporations, and federal, state, and local government agencies. Among the factors contributing to this growth is increased environmental, historic, and cultural preservation legislation. There is a particular demand for people with the ability to write environmental impact statements. There also is a growing need for anthropologists working for the U.S. Department of Defense and other areas of the federal government, assessing the customs and values of societies in specific regions of the world. Anthropologists will have to be creative in finding work outside of academia and convincing employers that their training in anthropology makes them uniquely qualified for the work. For these jobs, they will be competing with people from a variety of disciplines.

College and university teaching has traditionally been the largest area of employment for anthropologists, but it will be difficult to land a tenure-track position due to the fact that many anthropologists would like to work as educators. Overall, the number of job applicants will be greater than the number of openings available. Competition will be great even for those with doctorates who are seeking faculty positions, and many will find only temporary or nontenured jobs. Junior college and high school teaching jobs will be very limited, and those holding a bachelor's or master's degree will have few opportunities. Positions will be available in nonacademic areas, as well as a limited number in education.

FOR MORE INFORMATION

The following organization offers valuable information about anthropological careers and student associations:
American Anthropological Association
2200 Wilson Boulevard, Suite 600
Arlington, VA 22201-3357
Tel: 703-528-1902
http://www.aaanet.org

For information about anthropological genetics, contact
American Association of Anthropological Genetics
http://www.anthgen.org

For information on careers and a list of graduate programs in anthropology, contact
American Association of Physical Anthropologists
http://www.physanth.org

To learn more about the Student Challenge Awards and the other programs available, contact
Earthwatch Institute
114 Western Avenue
Boston, MA 02134-1037
Tel: 800-776-0188
E-mail: info@earthwatch.org
http://www.earthwatch.org

The SfAA Web site has career listings and publications for those wanting to read more about current topics in the social sciences. It also offers a list of colleges and universities that offer degrees in applied anthropology.
Society for Applied Anthropology (SfAA)
PO Box 2436
Oklahoma City, OK 73101-2436
Tel: 405-843-5113
E-mail: info@sfaa.net
http://www.sfaa.net

College Professors, Anthropology/ Archaeology

OVERVIEW

Professors instruct undergraduate and graduate students in the subjects of anthropology and archaeology at colleges and universities. They lecture classes, lead seminar groups, create and grade examinations, and oversee university-sponsored archaeological fieldwork. They also may conduct research, write for publication, and aid in administration. There are approximately 5,880 postsecondary anthropology and archaeology teachers in the United States.

HISTORY

The concept of colleges and universities goes back many centuries. These institutions evolved slowly from monastery schools, which trained a select few for certain professions, notably theology. The terms *college* and *university* have become virtually interchangeable in America outside the walls of academia, although originally they designated two very different kinds of institutions.

Two of the most notable early European universities were the University of Bologna in Italy, thought to have been established in the 12th century, and the University of Paris, which was chartered in 1201. These universities were considered to be models after which other European universities were patterned. Oxford University in England was probably established during the 12th century. Oxford served as a model for early American colleges and universities and today is still considered one of the world's leading institutions.

Harvard, the first U.S. college, was established in 1636. Its stated purpose was to train men for the ministry; the early colleges were all established for religious training. With the growth of state-supported institutions in the early 18th century, the process of freeing the curriculum from ties with the church began. The University of Virginia established the first liberal arts curriculum in 1825, and these innovations were later adopted by many other colleges and universities.

Although the original colleges in the United States were patterned after Oxford University, they later came under the influence of German universities. During the 19th century, more than 9,000 Americans went to Germany to study. The emphasis in German universities was on the scientific method. Most of the people who had studied in Germany returned to the United States to teach in universities, bringing this objective, factual approach to education and to other fields of learning.

In 1833, Oberlin College in Oberlin, Ohio, became the first college founded as a coeducational institution. In 1836, the first women-only college, Wesleyan Female College, was founded in Macon, Georgia.

The junior college movement in the United States has been one of the most rapidly growing educational developments. Junior colleges first came into being just after the turn of the 20th century.

The first anthropology-related coursework in the United States was offered at the University of Pennsylvania in 1886. (The university founded a formal department of anthropology in 1913.) Columbia University created the first academic department of anthropology in the United States in 1896. The department was led by Franz Boas, one of the founders of modern anthropology. Other major schools that offered early anthropology education were Harvard University, Clark University (which also conferred the first doctorate in the field in 1892), and the University of Chicago. But it was not until the 1920s and 1930s that anthropology (and its subfield of archaeology) became an established science. Archaeology departments are typically part of anthropology departments; few separate archaeology departments exist in U.S. colleges and universities. Today, more than 350 colleges and universities offer degree programs in anthropology/archaeology.

THE JOB

Anthropology and archaeology faculty members teach at junior colleges or at four-year colleges and universities. At four-year institutions, most faculty members are *assistant professors, associate professors,* or *full professors.* These three types of professorships differ in regards to status, job responsibilities, and salary. Assistant professors, also known as *adjunct professors,* are new faculty members who are working to get tenure (status as a permanent professor); they seek to advance to associate and then to full professorships.

Anthropology and archaeology professors perform three main functions: teaching, service, and research. Their most important responsibility is to teach students. Their role within the department will determine the level of courses they teach and the number of courses per semester. Most professors work with students at all levels, from college freshmen to graduate students. They may teach several classes a semester or only a few a year. Though professors may spend only 12 to 16 hours a week in the actual classroom, they spend many hours preparing lesson plans, grading assignments and exams, and preparing grade reports. They also schedule office or computer laboratory hours during the week to be available to students outside of regular classes, and they meet with students individually throughout the semester. In the classroom, professors lecture, lead discussions, administer exams, and assign textbook reading and other research. While most professors teach entry-level archaeology classes such as Introduction to Archaeology or Archaeological Theory and Methods, some also teach higher level classes that center on a particular specialty such as underwater archaeology, forensic archaeology, or Geographic Information Systems technology as it is applied to archaeology.

An important part of teaching is advising students. Not all faculty members serve as advisers, but those who do must set aside large blocks of time to guide students through the program. College professors who serve as advisers may have any number of students assigned to them, from fewer than 10 to more than 100, depending on the administrative policies of the college. Their responsibility may involve looking over a planned program of studies to make sure the students meet requirements for graduation, or it may involve working intensively with each student on many aspects of college life. They may also discuss the different fields of anthropology and archaeology with students and help them identify the best career choices.

All college professors provide important services to their department, college, or profession. Many college professors edit technical journal, review research and scholarship, and head committees about their field of expertise. College professors also serve on committees that determine the curriculum or make decisions about student learning.

The third responsibility of college and university faculty members is research and publication. Faculty members who are heavily involved in research programs sometimes are assigned a smaller teaching load. College anthropology and archaeology professors publish their research findings in various scholarly journals such as the *American Journal of Archaeology, The Institute of Nautical Archaeology Quarterly,* or the *Journal of Field Archaeology.* They may also write articles for publications such as *Archaeology* that are geared toward the public. They also write books based on their research or on their own knowledge and experience in the field. Most textbooks are written by college and university teachers, or practicing anthropologists and archaeologists. Publishing a significant amount of work has been the traditional standard by which assistant professors prove themselves worthy of becoming permanent, tenured faculty. Typically, pressure to publish is greatest for assistant professors. Pressure to publish increases again if an associate professor wishes to be considered for a promotion to full professorship.

In recent years, some liberal arts colleges have recognized that the pressure to publish is taking faculty away from their primary duties to the students, and these institutions have begun to place a decreasing emphasis on publishing and more on performance in the classroom. Professors in junior colleges face less pressure to publish than those in four-year institutions. Some faculty members eventually rise to the position of *department chair,* where they govern the affairs of an entire anthropology department. Department chairs, faculty, and other professional staff members are aided in their myriad duties by *graduate assistants,* who may help develop teaching materials, moderate laboratories, conduct research, give examinations, teach lower level courses, and carry out other activities.

Some college professors may also conduct classes in an extension program. In such a program, they teach evening and weekend courses for the benefit of people who otherwise would not be able to take advantage of the institution's resources. They may travel away from the campus and meet with a group of students at another location. They may work full time for the extension division or may divide their time between on-campus and off-campus teaching.

Distance learning programs, an increasingly popular option for students, give professors the opportunity to use today's technologies

Archaeology Glossaries on the Web

About.com: Archaeology Dictionary
http://archaeology.about.com/od/glossary/Archaeology_Diction
    ary_Index.htm

**Archaeological Institute of America: Introduction to Archaeology:
    Glossary**
http://www.archaeological.org/webinfo.php?page=10299

dig **glossary**
http://www.digonsite.com/glossary

Glossary of Archaeological Terms
http://www.enviro-explorers.com/glossary.html

Great Archaeology: Archaeology Glossary Terms
http://www.greatarchaeology.com/glossary.php

to remain in one place while teaching students who are at a variety of locations simultaneously. The professor's duties, like those when teaching correspondence courses conducted by mail, include grading work that students send in at periodic intervals and advising students of their progress. Computers, the Internet, e-mail, and video conferencing, however, are some of the technology tools that allow professors and students to communicate in "real time" in a virtual classroom setting. Meetings may be scheduled during the same time as traditional classes or during evenings and weekends. Professors who do this work are sometimes known as *extension work, correspondence, distance learning,* or *online instructors.* They may teach online courses in addition to other classes or may have distance learning as their major teaching responsibility.

The *junior college instructor* has many of the same kinds of responsibilities as does the teacher in a four-year college or university. Because junior colleges offer only a two-year program, they teach only undergraduates.

REQUIREMENTS
High School
Your high school's college preparatory program likely includes courses in English, science, foreign language, history, math, and

A professor of archaeology at the University of Denver (*left*) reads a Ground Penetrating Radar (GPR) computer monitor as a volunteer archaeology graduate student pulls the GPR antennae in New York's Central Park. Archaeologists are using this technology to try to learn more about Seneca Village, a vanished 19th-century settlement. (*Mary Altaffer, AP Photo*)

government. In addition, you should take courses in speech to get a sense of what it will be like to lecture to a group of students. Your school's debate team can also help you develop public speaking skills, along with research skills. Your high school may even offer introductory courses in anthropology or archaeology. If so, take as many of these as possible.

Postsecondary Training

At least one advanced degree in your field of study (anthropology, archaeology, or related subfields such as environmental archaeology or cultural anthropology) is required to be a professor in a college or university. The master's degree is considered the minimum standard, and graduate work beyond the master's is usually desirable. If you hope to advance in academic rank above instructor, most institutions require a doctorate.

In the last year of your undergraduate program, you'll apply to graduate programs in your area of study. Standards for admission to a graduate program can be high and the competition heavy, depending on the school. Once accepted into a program, your responsibilities will be similar to those of your professors—in addition to attending seminars, you'll research, prepare articles for publication, and teach some undergraduate courses.

You may find employment in a junior college with only a master's degree. Advancement in responsibility and in salary, however, is more likely to come if you have earned a doctorate.

Other Requirements

You should enjoy reading, writing, and researching. Not only will you spend many years studying in school, your whole career will be based on communicating your thoughts and ideas. People skills are important because you'll be dealing directly with students, administrators, and other faculty members on a daily basis. You should feel comfortable in a role of authority and possess self-confidence.

EXPLORING

Your high school teachers use many of the same skills as college professors, so talk to your teachers about their careers and their college experiences. You can develop your own teaching experience by volunteering at a community center, working at a day care center, or working at a summer camp. Also, spend some time on a college campus to get a sense of the environment. Write to colleges for their admissions brochures and course catalogs (or check them out online). Visit the Web sites of college departments of anthropology/archaeology to read about majors, typical courses, and faculty members. Before visiting college campuses, make arrangements to speak to professors who teach courses that interest you. These professors may allow you to sit in on their classes and observe. Also, make appointments with college advisers and with people in the admissions and recruitment offices. If your grades are good enough, you might be able to serve as a teaching assistant during your undergraduate years, which can give you experience leading discussions and grading papers.

Learn as much as you can about anthropology and archaeology. Read books and magazines about these fields and try to arrange information interviews with anthropologists and archaeologists to learn about career paths and work settings. You can also visit Web sites such as Frequently Asked Questions About a Career in Archaeology in the U.S. (http://www.museum.state.il.us/ismdepts/anthro/dlcfaq.html).

EMPLOYERS

Approximately 5,880 postsecondary anthropology and archaeology teachers are employed in the United States. Employment opportunities vary based on area of study and education. With a doctorate, a number of publications, and a record of good teaching, professors should find opportunities in universities all across the country. Professors teach in undergraduate and graduate programs. The teaching jobs at doctoral institutions are usually better paying and more prestigious. The most sought-after positions are those that offer tenure. Teachers that have only a master's degree will be limited to opportunities with junior colleges, community colleges, and some small private institutions.

STARTING OUT

You should start the process of finding a teaching position while you are in graduate school. The process includes developing a curriculum vitae (a detailed, academic resume), writing for publication, assisting with research, attending conferences, and gaining teaching experience and recommendations. Many students begin applying for teaching positions while finishing their graduate program. For most positions at four-year institutions, you must travel to large conferences where interviews can be arranged with representatives from the universities to which you have applied.

Because of the competition for tenure-track positions, you may have to work for a few years in temporary positions, visiting various schools as a postdoctoral researcher or as an adjunct professor. Some professional associations maintain lists of teaching opportunities in their areas. They may also make lists of applicants available to college administrators looking to fill an available position. These lists are also often available on the associations' Web sites. The College and University Professional Association for Human Resources, for example, maintains a job list at its Web site, http://www.cupahr.org. Another resource is *The Chronicle of Higher Education* (http://www.chronicle.com), a newspaper with national job listings that is available in print and online.

Some professors begin teaching after having successful careers as anthropologists or archaeologists.

ADVANCEMENT

The normal pattern of advancement is from instructor to assistant professor, to associate professor, to full professor. All four academic ranks are concerned primarily with teaching and research. College faculty members who have an interest in and a talent for administration may advance to department chair or dean of their college. A few become college or university presidents or other types of administrators.

The instructor is usually an inexperienced college teacher. He or she may hold a doctorate or may have completed all the Ph.D. requirements except for the dissertation. Some colleges look upon the rank of instructor as the period during which the college is trying out the teacher. Instructors are advanced to the position of assistant professor within three to four years. Assistant professors are given up to approximately six years to prove themselves worthy of tenure, and if they do so, they become associate professors. Some professors choose to remain at the associate level. Others strive to become full professors and receive greater status, salary, and responsibilities.

Most colleges have clearly defined promotion policies from rank to rank for faculty members, and many have written statements about the number of years in which instructors and assistant professors may remain in grade. Administrators in many colleges hope to encourage younger faculty members to increase their skills and competencies and thus to qualify for the more responsible positions of associate professor and full professor.

EARNINGS

According to the U.S. Department of Labor, in 2009, postsecondary anthropology and archaeology teachers earned median annual salaries of $69,520, with 10 percent earning $119,070 or more and 10 percent earning $41,270 or less. Those with the highest earnings tend to be senior tenured faculty; those with the lowest, graduate assistants. Professors working on the West Coast and the East Coast and those working at doctorate-granting institutions also tend to earn the highest salaries. Many professors try to increase their earnings by completing research, publishing in their field, or teaching additional courses.

Benefits for full-time faculty typically include health insurance and retirement funds and, in some cases, stipends for travel related to research, housing allowances, and tuition waivers for dependents.

WORK ENVIRONMENT

A college or university is usually a pleasant place in which to work. Campuses bustle with all types of activities and events, stimulating ideas, and a young, energetic population. Much prestige comes with success as a professor and scholar; professors have the respect of students, colleagues, and others in their community.

Depending on the size of the department, professors may have their own office, or they may have to share an office with one or more colleagues. Their department may provide them with a computer, Internet access, and research assistants. College professors are also able to do much of their office work at home. They can arrange their schedule around class hours, academic meetings, and the established office hours when they meet with students. Most teachers work more than 40 hours each week. Although professors may teach only two or three classes a semester, they spend many hours preparing for lectures and computer labs, examining student work, and conducting research.

OUTLOOK

The U.S. Department of Labor predicts faster than average employment growth for college and university professors through 2018. College enrollment is projected to grow due to an increased number of 18- to 24-year-olds, an increased number of adults returning to college, and an increased number of foreign-born students. Retirement of current faculty members will also provide job openings. However, competition for full-time, tenure-track positions at four-year schools will be very strong.

Employment for anthropology and archaeology educators will not be as strong. There is little turnover in the field and aspiring professors will find it difficult to land a tenure-track position. More opportunities will be found at community colleges and in high schools.

FOR MORE INFORMATION

The following organization offers valuable information about anthropological careers and student associations:
American Anthropological Association
2200 Wilson Boulevard, Suite 600
Arlington, VA 22201-3357
Tel: 703-528-1902
http://www.aaanet.org

For information on careers and a list of graduate programs in physical anthropology, contact
American Association of Physical Anthropologists
http://www.physanth.org

To read about the issues affecting college professors, contact the following organizations:

American Association of University Professors
1133 19th Street, NW, Suite 200
Washington, DC 20036-3655
Tel: 202-737-5900
E-mail: aaup@aaup.org
http://www.aaup.org

American Federation of Teachers
555 New Jersey Avenue, NW
Washington, DC 20001-2029
Tel: 202-879-4400
http://www.aft.org

The association represents the interests of women in higher education. Visit its Web site for information on scholarships for college students and AAUW Outlook.

American Association of University Women (AAUW)
1111 16th Street, NW
Washington, DC 20036-4809
Tel: 800-326-2289
E-mail: connect@aauw.org
http://www.aauw.org

For information on archaeological careers and job listings, contact

Society for American Archaeology
900 Second Street, NE, Suite 12
Washington, DC 20002-3560
Tel: 202-789-8200
E-mail: headquarters@saa.org
http://www.saa.org

The SfAA Web site has career listings and publications for those wanting to read more about current topics in the social sciences. It also offers a list of colleges and universities that offer degrees in applied anthropology.

Society for Applied Anthropology (SfAA)
PO Box 2436
Oklahoma City, OK 73101-2436
Tel: 405-843-5113
E-mail: info@sfaa.net
http://www.sfaa.net

For career information, contact
Society for Historical Archaeology
9707 Key West Avenue, Suite 100
Rockville, MD 20850-3992
Tel: 301-990-2454
E-mail: hq@sha.org
http://www.sha.org
http://www.sha.org/EHA/splash.cfm

Conservators and Conservation Technicians

OVERVIEW

Conservators analyze and assess the condition of artifacts and pieces of art, plan for the care of collections, and carry out conservation treatments and programs. Conservators may be in private practice or work for museums, historical societies, or state institutions. When conserving artifacts or artwork, these professionals must select methods and materials that preserve and retain the original integrity of each piece. Conservators must be knowledgeable about the objects in their care, which may be natural objects, such as bones and fossils, or man-made objects, such as artifacts, paintings, photographs, sculpture, paper, and metal.

Conservation technicians work under the supervision of conservators and complete maintenance work on the collection.

HISTORY

The earliest written records of antiquities being conserved date from the first century A.D., but the methods of conservation that were used are unknown. According to the International Institute for Conservation of Historic and Artistic Works, the seeds of modern conservation were planted during the Renaissance as a result of archaeological excavations at Pompeii and Herculaneum that led to a need to preserve archaeological finds. In the late 1700s and early 1800s interest grew in the proper conservation of archaeological

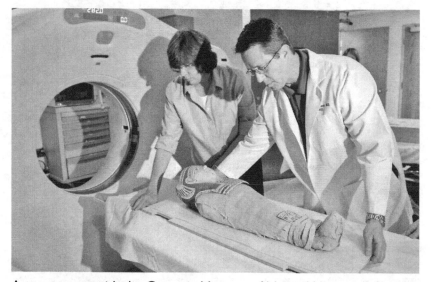

A conservator with the Carnegie Museum of Natural History (*left*) helps the chief of musculoskeletal imaging at the University of Pittsburgh School of Medicine prepare a mummy that dates back to Egypt's Ptolemaic Dynasty for a CT scan. Based on the CT scan, researchers believe the child was a boy around five years old. (*Justin Merriman, AP Photo*/Pittsburgh Tribune-Review)

objects. Conservation as we known it today emerged in the early decades of the 20th century as researchers and archaeologists worked to develop methods to best conserve artifacts.

Conservators today use highly scientific methods and recognize the need both to care for objects before deterioration occurs and to treat objects after damage has been done.

The first regional conservation laboratory in the United States, known as the Intermuseum Conservation Association, was created in 1952 in Oberlin, Ohio, when several smaller museums joined to bring their skills together.

Thanks to increasingly precise cleaning methods and scientific inventions, the science of archaeological conservation has advanced. Today, the field is highly specialized and those who work in it must face demanding standards and challenges.

THE JOB

Conservation professionals generally choose to specialize in one area of work defined by medium, such as in the preservation of statues, textiles, wooden artifacts, paintings, photographic materials, books and paper, or architecture. There are also conservators who specialize in archaeology or ethnographic materials, including tools (awls, axes, scrapers, etc.), clothing, weapons (knives, shields, spears, arrowheads, atlatls, etc.), and everyday items (pottery, saddles, etc.) that are made of stone, ceramics, leather, glass, bone, or other resources. Many conservation professionals are employed by museums, while others provide services through private practice. Common conservation issues associated with archaeological artifacts include metal objects that are corroded or cracked; ceramic objects that are cracked, crumbling, or flaking, damaged by salt, or stained by the presence of metals or other materials; glass objects that are pitted, cracked, or otherwise damaged or decaying; bone objects that have been damaged by water or breakage; wood objects that are waterlogged or that have been inundated with biological growth; leather objects that are worn or torn, stained, under biological attack (by molds, bacteria, or insects), been damaged by water, or chemically deteriorating; paper that is physically damaged, oxidizing, or affected by biological activity; and human remains that are under attack from biological agents or damaged in other ways. Other artifacts that conservators and conservation technicians may work with include shell, horn, tortoiseshell, rubber, and plastic.

Conservation activities include carrying out technical and scientific studies on art objects, stabilizing the structure and reintegrating the appearance of cultural artifacts, and establishing the environment in which artifacts are best preserved. A conservator's responsibilities also may include documenting the structure and condition of objects through written and visual recording, designing programs for preventive care, and executing conservation treatments. Conservation tools include microscopes and cameras and equipment for specialized processes such as infrared and ultraviolet photography and X-rays.

Conservation technicians assist conservators in preserving or restoring artifacts and art objects. To do this, they study descriptions and information about the object and may perform chemical and physical tests and treatments as specified by the conservator. For example, after a broken and discolored 2,000-year-old Anasazi ceramic is recovered at an archaeological site, the technician will first clean the item gently using a brush with soft bristles and deionized water. (Ceramics that are in extremely fragile shape—crumbling bodies or flaking paint or glaze—are not cleaned in this manner.) After allowing the ceramic pieces to completely dry, the technician mends them together using a conservation-grade adhesive (with the type chosen varying by the type of ceramic, its condition, and the long-term conservation plan for the object). The technician may also fill gaps in the ceramic using Plaster of Paris, dental plaster, or other compounds.

Some conservators and conservation technicians work in the field at archaeological sites. They are present if archaeologists anticipate that they will make a unique find, be working in waterlogged sites, or working with fragile artifacts that may be seriously degraded or corroded. Conservators and conservation technicians may also work "on call" for an archaeological excavation and only come to the site when their particular talents are needed.

There are several other specialties for conservation professionals. A *conservation scientist* is a professional scientist whose primary focus is in developing materials and knowledge to support conservation activities. Some specialize in scientific research into art materials, such as paints and varnishes, or firing methods and building materials of ceramics. *Conservation educators* have substantial knowledge and experience in the theory and practice of conservation and have chosen to direct their efforts toward teaching the principles, methodology, and technical aspects of the profession. *Preparators* supervise the installation of specimens, art objects, and artifacts, often working with design technicians, curators, and directors to ensure the safety and preservation of items on display.

REQUIREMENTS

High School

Good conservation work comes from a well-balanced formulation of art and science. To prepare for a career in conservation, concentrate on doing well in all academic subjects, including courses in chemistry, natural science, history, and the arts. Speech and English courses will help you to develop your communication skills.

Postsecondary Training

In the past, many conservation professionals received their training solely through apprenticeships with esteemed conservators. The same is not true today; you will need a bachelor's degree to find work as a technician, and in all but the smallest institutions you will need a master's degree to advance to conservator. Because graduate programs are highly selective, you should plan your academic path with care.

At the undergraduate level, take course work in the sciences, including inorganic and organic chemistry, the humanities (art history, archaeology, and anthropology), and studio art. Some graduate programs will consider work experience and gained expertise in conservation practice as comparable to course work when screening applicants. In addition, most graduate programs recognize a student's participation in apprenticeship or internship positions while also completing course work as an indication of the applicant's commitment to the career.

Other Requirements
Conservation can be physically demanding. Conservators and conservation technicians must concentrate on specific physical and mental tasks for long periods of time. Endurance, manual dexterity, and patience are often needed to complete projects successfully. Conservation professionals also must be highly organized and be willing to continue to learn throughout their careers. Conservation technicians must be able to follow instructions and work productively on their own when necessary.

EXPLORING

If you are considering a career in the conservation of artifacts or art, try contacting local museums or conservation laboratories that may allow tours or interviews. Read trade or technical journals to gain a sense of the many issues that conservators address. Contact professional organizations, such as the American Institute for Conservation of Historic and Artistic Works, for directories of training and conservation programs and career information.

Because employment in this field, even at the entry level, most often entails handling precious materials and cultural resources, you should be fairly well prepared before contacting professionals to request either an internship or a volunteer position. You need to demonstrate a high level of academic achievement and have a serious interest in the career to edge out the competition for a limited number of jobs.

EMPLOYERS

Museums, libraries, historical societies, private conservation laboratories, contract archaeology companies, and government agencies hire conservators and conservation technicians. Institutions with small operating budgets sometimes hire part-time specialists to perform conservation work. This is especially common when curators need extra help in preparing items for display. Antique dealers may also seek the expertise of an experienced conservator for merchandise restoration, identification, and appraisal purposes.

The U.S. Department of Labor reports that an increasing number of conservators are becoming self-employed as a result of more museums hiring these workers on a contract basis.

STARTING OUT

Most often students entering the field of conservation have completed high school and undergraduate studies, and many are contemplating graduate programs. At this point a student is ready to seek a position (often unpaid) as an apprentice or intern with either a private conservation company or a museum to gain a practical feel for the work. Training opportunities are scarce and in high demand. Prospective students must convince potential trainers of their dedication to the highly demanding craft of conservation. The combination of academic or formal training along with hands-on experience and apprenticeship is the ideal foundation for entering the career.

ADVANCEMENT

Due to rapid changes in each conservation specialty, practicing conservators must keep abreast of advances in technology and methodology. Conservators stay up to date by reading publications, attending professional meetings, and enrolling in short-term workshops or courses.

An experienced conservator wishing to move into another realm of the field may become a private consultant, an appraiser of art or artifacts, a conservation educator, a curator, or a museum registrar.

EARNINGS

Salaries for conservators vary greatly depending on the level of experience, chosen specialty, region, job description, and employer. The U.S. Department of Labor, which classifies conservators with curators, museum technicians, and archivists, reports the median annual earnings for this group as $37,120 in 2009. The lowest paid 10 percent of this group earned less than $23,530, and the highest paid 10 percent made more than $67,090.

According to the American Institute for Conservation of Historic and Artistic Works 2009 compensation report, depending on the employer a first-year conservator working full time can expect to earn approximately $24,250 to $61,250 annually. Full-time conservators with several years of experience report annual earnings between $12,250 and $111,500 with a median of $40,000. Senior conservators have reported earnings between $25,640 and $112,000 with median earnings of $46,800 annually.

Fringe benefits, including paid vacations, medical and dental insurance, sick leave, and retirement plans, vary according to each employer's policies.

WORK ENVIRONMENT

Conservation work may be conducted indoors in laboratories or at an archaeological site. Conservators typically work 40 to 60 hours per week depending on exhibit schedules and deadlines, as well as the amount and condition of unstable objects in their collections. Because some conservation tasks and techniques involve the use of toxic chemicals, laboratories are equipped with ventilation systems. At times a conservator may find it necessary to wear a mask and possibly even a respirator when working with particularly harsh chemicals or varnishes. Most of the work requires meticulous attention to detail, a great deal of precision, and manual dexterity.

The rewards of the conservation profession are the satisfaction of preserving artifacts that reflect the diversity of human achievements; being in regular contact with art, artifacts, and structures; enjoying a stimulating workplace; and the creative application of expertise to the preservation of artistically and historically significant objects.

OUTLOOK

The U.S. Department of Labor predicts that employment for museum conservators and technicians will grow much faster than the average for all careers through 2018. Competition for these desirable positions, however, will be strong. Conservators who speak a foreign language and who are willing to travel will have the best employment prospects.

The public's developing interest in cultural material of all forms will contribute to conservation and preservation as a growing field. New specialties have emerged in response to the interest in collections maintenance and preventive care. Conservation, curatorial, and registration responsibilities are intermingling and creating hybrid conservation professional titles, such as collections care, environmental monitoring, and exhibits specialists.

Despite these developments, however, any decreases in federal funding often affect employment and educational opportunities. For example, in any given year, if Congress limits government assistance to the National Endowment for the Arts, less money is available to assist students through unpaid internships. As museums experience a tightening of federal funds, many may choose to decrease the number of paid conservators on staff and instead may rely on a small staff augmented by private conservation companies that can be contracted on a short-term basis as necessary. Private industry and for-profit companies will then continue to grow, while federally funded nonprofit museums may experience a reduction of staff.

FOR MORE INFORMATION

For additional information on conservation careers and training, contact

American Institute for Conservation of Historic and Artistic Works
1156 15th Street, NW, Suite 320
Washington DC 20005-1714
Tel: 202-452-9545
E-mail: info@conservation-us.org
http://www.conservation-us.org

For information about conservation and training, contact

International Centre for the Study of the Preservation and Restoration of Cultural Property
Via di San Michele 13
I-00153 Rome, Italy
E-mail: iccrom@iccrom.org
http://www.iccrom.org

For more information about conservation and publications, contact

International Institute for Conservation of Historic and Artistic Works
6 Buckingham Street
WC2N 6BA London, United Kingdom
E-mail: iic@iiconservation.org
http://www.iiconservation.org

For information on preservation training, contact

National Center for Preservation Technology and Training
National Park Service
645 University Parkway
Natchitoches, LA 71457-3913
Tel: 318-356-7444
E-mail: ncptt@nps.gov
http://www.ncptt.nps.gov

RAP is a "national network of nonprofit organizations with expertise in the field of conservation and preservation." Visit its Web site for more information.
Regional Alliance for Preservation (RAP)
http://www.rap-arcc.org

Visit the society's Web site to read Conservation FAQs and Facts.
Society for Historical Archaeology
9707 Key West Avenue, Suite 100
Rockville, MD 20850-3992
Tel: 301-990-2454
E-mail: hq@sha.org
http://www.sha.org/research_resources/conservation_faqs/
    default.cfm

For information on internships and other learning opportunities in Canada, contact
Canadian Conservation Institute
1030 Innes Road
Ottawa ON K1A 0M5 Canada
Tel: 613-998-3721
http://www.cci-icc.gc.ca

INTERVIEW

Lynn Grant is a senior conservator at the University of Pennsylvania Museum of Archaeology and Anthropology in Philadelphia. She discussed her career with the editors of Careers in Focus: Archaeology.

Q. What made you want to enter this career?
A. For a long time I didn't even know such a career existed. I was fascinated by the objects that people made and used in the past and I started out thinking I wanted to be an archaeologist. As I learned more about archaeology, I came to understand that archaeologists didn't really spend much of their time with the artifacts, which is where my true interest was. Finally, a former professor who had just met a conservator called me and said: "I know what you want to be." When she described the profession, I realized it was what I'd been looking for all along without knowing it. I get to interact with wonderful artifacts

that tell us about the people who made and used them; it's like a direct link to people who may have lived thousands of years ago. When I'm examining a 1,300-year-old Maya pottery vessel and see the potter's fingerprint preserved in the clay slip, it's like he (or she) is speaking to me.

Q. Please describe a day in your life on the job. What are your typical responsibilities? Can you describe your work environment?

A. Every day is different, which is one thing I like about my job. I can be working on one particular object, getting it ready for exhibit, or helping to ensure that a whole collection of artifacts is kept in the best possible conditions to promote their stability. Conservation breaks down into two main modes: active and passive. Active conservation is where you actually interact with the artifact: cleaning, mending, or stabilizing it, but that's only one small portion of our responsibility. Passive conservation (also known as preventative conservation) is controlling the artifact's whole environment to preserve it as long as possible. This includes how objects are stored, how they are exhibited, how they can be handled; things as complex as controlling the humidity in a storeroom or as simple as ensuring that textiles are rolled properly. My work environment includes office space, with a computer and files, plus a large lab and workroom. I also sometimes have to go to where the artifacts are—in the galleries or the storerooms—rather than bringing them to the lab. It depends on what's best for the artifact.

Q. What are the most important personal and professional qualities for conservators?

A. Conservators are generalists, who have to know something about a lot of different areas: art, craft, chemistry, physics, materials science, construction, and even diplomacy (it's not always easy to say "no, you can't do that to that artifact" but that's often the conservator's job). Most conservators I know are very balanced between lateral and linear thinking; equally "right-brained" and "left-brained." Apart from that, one of the most important qualities is enormous amounts of patience. Much of what we do can be extremely tedious (rolling tiny cotton swabs across a dirty surface for hours and hours and hours) but you can't let your attention lag even on the 3,000th swab. Pattern recognition is another important skill—the kind of thing that makes one good at jigsaw puzzles. The ability to think creatively—to come up with new solutions for new challenges is also important. Professional ethics are a very important criterion for conservators; we have the ability to change how people perceive the past by how we present its artifacts. It's important not to let your work obscure that of the original maker or user of the artifact.

Q. What are some of the pros and cons of your job?

A. The pros are easy: we get to work with some of the most wonderful artifacts in human history, giving them new life. The thrill of working on something that was made 4,000 years ago halfway around the world just doesn't ever go away. We also get to work with a whole array of fascinating specialists: curators, researchers, exhibit designers, engineers, artists, students, etc. It's really fun to see how different people react to the same artifact.

The cons are harder: Sometimes I feel as though my job is to be the person who says "No": "No, you can't have a dance party in the museum gallery," "No, that object is too fragile to be loaned," "No, you can't turn up the lights in the galleries because it will damage the artifacts," "No, you shouldn't store those artifacts there." It can be a hard position to be in. This is another area where creative thinking comes in handy: if you can say "no" to an idea by offering a better alternative.

Q. What is the employment outlook for conservators?

A. There's always a need for conservators; there isn't always the money to hire them. Most institutions that employ conservators are nonprofit museums, galleries, and the like and such places are always dependent on public funding. Young conservators, especially, may need to be willing to go where jobs are rather than relying on finding one where they want to live. This is a career that one goes into for love not money.

Q. What advice would you give to young people who want to become conservators?

A. Get as wide an experience as you can: try all sorts of different arts and crafts (such as jewelry making, ceramics, needlework). If you're art-oriented, made sure you balance that with enough science; if you're a natural scientist, make sure you do lots of things requiring hand skills. The road to be becoming a conservator can be long and winding but it's a great journey.

Cultural Resources Law Enforcement Officers

OVERVIEW

Cultural resources law enforcement officers, sometimes called *enforcement rangers,* protect archaeological sites at local, state, and national parks and other locations. They also work for agencies that investigate and prosecute those who engage in the unlawful trade of protected archaeological objects and remains.

HISTORY

Our nation's public lands are rich in archaeological treasures—from ancient Anasazi cliff dwellings in the American Southwest, to Revolutionary and Civil War battlefields, to a vast array of other prehistoric and historic sites. Unfortunately, through the years, many people have sought to get rich by stealing these treasures and selling them illegally. Sites were frequently looted by "amateur archaeologists," and scientific study was largely unregulated and unmonitored.

In 1849, the Department of the Interior was founded to protect federal lands—many of which contained priceless archaeological sites. But the department managed a vast area of land and did not have enough staffing to ensure that all archaeological sites were protected. Despite growing public and government interest in protecting these resources, looting continued, and just one site, the Casa Grande Ruins in Arizona, was protected for archaeological study.

It was not until the passage of the Antiquities Act in 1906 by Congress that government-owned archaeological sites began receiving strong protection. The act, according to the National Park Service, "decreed presidential authority to establish National Monuments and required permits to be approved before archaeological investigations could be undertaken on federal land." The Antiquities Act marks the beginning of organized protection of cultural resources by the federal government. Many new parks and monuments were created, and in 1916 the National Park Service was founded to oversee these sites. In the following decades, other agencies, as well as advocacy organizations, were created to manage and conserve federal lands, including the Bureau of Land Management (1946) and the National Trust for Historic Preservation (1949).

Over the years, several important laws have been enacted to further protect archaeological and cultural resources, including the Archaeological Resources Protection Act (1979) and the Native American Graves Protection and Repatriation Act (1990). In 2009, the National Landscape Conservation System was established. It is a 26-million acre collection of the best national monuments, historic sites, wilderness areas, scenic rivers, and trails in the American West.

Today, law enforcement officers are employed at local, state, and national parks to protect archaeological resources and allow them to be studied and enjoyed by future generations.

Cultural resources law enforcement officers are also employed in nearly every country throughout the world. Some countries—such as Italy and Egypt—even have their own archaeology or cultural resources police forces that investigate theft of cultural resources and monitor sites so that theft or vandalism does not occur.

THE JOB

Although the actual job titles of cultural resources law enforcement officers may vary by employer, they largely perform similar duties. In short, they protect and monitor cultural and archaeological resources on public lands—ranging from Native American ruins and petroglyphs, battlefields, historic structures, historic trails, and any other area that is deemed to be of cultural value. They carry weapons and receive advanced training in their appropriate use. Most officers, except for special agents, wear uniforms. In addition to protecting cultural resources, many law enforcement officers are also responsible for protecting natural resources, safeguarding visitors and staff, providing emergency medical services, conducting wilderness rescues, and overseeing special park uses, such as commercial filming.

Law enforcement officers patrol the vast expanses of our nation's hundreds of millions of acres of public lands. In order to perform their duties, they must spend a great deal of time in the field. Fieldwork may involve hiking trails, patrolling an area's waters in boats, or interacting with visitors. They spend a considerable amount of time traveling through their park or enforcement area to ensure that illegal acts are not being committed. Officers may also guard archaeological and cultural resources that are on display at museums and visitor centers in parks and on other public lands.

There are two types of people who come to public lands: tourists and looters, and officers approach these groups in different ways. The average tourist visits a park to enjoy its natural and historical wonders and may be unaware of laws relating to cultural resources. It is the job of the law enforcement officer to educate them about these laws. For example, visitors may be unaware that it is illegal to remove artifacts or human remains from protected areas. If an officer encounters a visitor in the process of removing an artifact, he or she will confiscate the artifact and turn it over to the park's archaeologist. Artifacts and cultural resources may also be intentionally or unintentionally damaged by visitors. For example, they may enter prohibited areas and damage resources, deface petroglyphs and pictographs, or vandalize ruins or historical buildings. If the officer catches an individual committing a criminal act, he or she will arrest them or issue a citation, depending on the severity of the damage. If the officer discovers damage to archaeological and cultural resources after the fact, he or she notifies the park's head archaeologist and conservator so that repairs can be made.

Looters are a major problem on government-owned lands. They are criminals who knowingly break the law to gather artifacts (arrowheads, pottery, headdresses, ceramics, bullet casings, weapons, petroglyphs, etc.) for illegal resale. They often dig in the ground to extract artifacts at sites—destroying the archaeological record forever. They may break off chunks of rocks that contain petroglyphs or simply pick up artifacts that have weathered up to the surface. Looting of archaeological and cultural sites has taken place since the early days of the United States, but, in recent years, it has become highly organized due to the high prices many artifacts fetch on the black market. The American Southwest has an especially high concentration of archaeological sites, and looting has become a major issue for cultural resources law enforcement officers. In fact, *Archaeology* magazine reports that the growing public addiction to methamphetamines, a highly addictive drug, is causing many addicts to loot archaeological sites in the Southwest and other areas to fund their addictions. These addicts completely destroy sites and remove every possible artifact, regardless of value. Methamphetamine users often exhibit agitated and violent behavior, which is making the policing of archaeological sites more dangerous. *Archaeology* magazine reports that the illegal drug/looting connection is not just occurring in the United States, but in countries throughout the world.

Cultural resources law enforcement officers must monitor archaeological sites day and night to ensure that looters do not steal our nation's cultural heritage. If they catch looters in the act, they observe the perpetrators and document their actions. Then the officers approach and attempt to arrest the suspects. They may have to chase the looters if they try to escape. At times, these situations can be highly dangerous, with looters shooting at officers or otherwise resisting arrest. If officers discover that an archaeological site has been looted, they quickly cordon off the area for investigation and call an archaeologist to the scene. They gather evidence in order to try to apprehend the looters. When officers apprehend suspected looters, they arrest them and file charges against them. Officers may be required to testify against the accused parties in court.

Officers also work on Native American reservations, which are sovereign nations according to U.S. law. They police archaeological sites and cultural areas and apprehend looters and others who damage sites.

Even the Federal Bureau of Investigation (FBI) plays a role in combating theft of antiquities. It has an Art Crime Team staffed with 13 special agents to investigate and apprehend people who steal cultural treasures. They receive special training and participate in investigations in the United States and worldwide. The FBI reports that the Art Crime Team has recovered more than 1,000 cultural items with a value exceeding $135 million since its founding in 2004. Some of the archaeological and cultural items recovered include more than 800 pre-Columbian artifacts stolen from Panama and Ecuador and two 15th-century maps stolen from the National Library in Spain.

The Bureau of Land Management (BLM) also employs special agents to apprehend those who loot or otherwise damage archaeological sites on BLM land. According to the BLM, they are responsible for "conducting complex investigations requiring the use of plainclothes/undercover operations, targeted surveillance, developing informants, serving search warrants, providing liaison with criminal justice officials, apprehending violators through criminal complaints and/or making arrests, and providing technical assistance to BLM rangers."

Although not sworn law enforcement officers in most cases, *museum guards* also protect archaeological and cultural resources. They patrol museums to ensure that artifacts are not damaged or stolen. Guards work during regular exhibition hours and at night and on weekends.

REQUIREMENTS

High School

Students who hope to work as cultural resources law enforcement officers should study history and archaeology during high school. They should also take classes that help them develop their communication skills. Because interaction with the public is such a significant part of this career, students may want to take psychology, education, and sociology courses. Students should also take physical education courses; physical fitness is a definite asset for people who must hike miles of backcountry trails to protect cultural resources.

Hands-on experience can be a distinct advantage for a person who is trying to enter a competitive field. Students who are interested in working for the National Park Service should seek this experience by volunteering for a national park, through the Volunteers-in-Parks (VIP) program (http://www.nps.gov/gettinginvolved/volunteer). Park volunteers can help park employees in any number of ways, including answering phone calls, welcoming visitors, maintaining trails, building fences, painting buildings, or picking up litter. Volunteer opportunities also are available at state and local parks.

Postsecondary Training

Some local government agencies may only require officers to have a high school diploma, but most require that officers have at least some college training. Many federal agencies prefer applicants to have a bachelor's degree in criminal justice along with course work in archaeology, history, law, or historic preservation.

Because there is so much competition for law enforcement jobs, especially those with federal agencies, many people put themselves through additional training programs to distinguish themselves from other candidates. Some undergo medical technician training programs or police academies. Others attend independent ranger academies to learn the fundamentals of law enforcement and emergency procedures. These training programs can offer an excellent foundation for a prospective law enforcement officer.

Once hired, federal law enforcement officers receive training at the Federal Law Enforcement Training Center (FLETC). Current officers also participate in specialized training regarding the protection of archaeological resources. The Archaeological Resources Protection Training Program was created by the FLETC in cooperation with the National Park Service, U.S. Forest

Service, and the Bureau of Land Management. During the five-day program, archaeologists and law enforcement officers participate in integrated lectures and discussions to learn about issues in the field. Then the two occupational groups are separated, with the archaeologists learning about law enforcement issues and the law enforcement officers focusing on archaeology- and law enforcement-related topics. The groups are then recombined and participate in a 12-hour practical exercise in which they investigate and document an archaeological crime scene.

Certification or Licensing
There is no general certification requirement for law enforcement officers. Individuals who become rangers may be given emergency medical training. Rangers who work in parks that have underwater archaeological resources may become certified divers.

Other Requirements
Law enforcement officers must be able to convey authority to individuals who are violating laws. Because of the stressful nature of much law enforcement work, they must be able to think clearly and logically during emergency situations, have a strong degree of emotional control, and be capable of detaching oneself from incidents. Officers also interact frequently with visitors. They must be friendly, confident, and able to communicate clearly.

Physical fitness training is a must for success in this career. Law enforcement officers must hike long distances to patrol large areas. They may have to climb mountains, wade streams, hike through tall grasses or over rocky areas, chase suspects on foot, and otherwise engage in strenuous activity. For many positions, applicants must be U.S. citizens.

EMPLOYERS

Cultural resources law enforcement officers are employed by federal, state, and local government agencies that manage public land. Federal agencies that employ law enforcement officers who protect archaeological and cultural resources include the National Park Service, the U.S. Forestry Service, the Bureau of Land Management, the U.S. Fish and Wildlife Service, the Federal Bureau of Investigation, and the Bureau of Indian Affairs. Cultural resources law enforcement officers also work for tribal governments. Security guards are employed by museums and cultural centers.

The skills necessary to many positions within the local, state, and national parks, forests, and other government land holdings also are highly transferable. Law enforcement rangers may consider careers as police officers, fire fighters, or emergency medical personnel.

STARTING OUT

If you are interested in applying for a federal law enforcement job, contact your local Federal Job Information Center or the federal Office of Personnel Management (http://www.usajobs.gov) for application information. Those who are interested in working at agencies at the local and state level should contact these agencies directly for employment information.

ADVANCEMENT

As is true of most professions, advancement for law enforcement officers usually means assuming managerial and administrative responsibilities. Rangers may become subdistrict rangers, district rangers, and then chief rangers. While this is the traditional path to advancement, it is not one that anyone treads very quickly. The opportunities for upward mobility within parks, national forests, and other protected areas are limited because the turnover rates at upper levels tend to be quite low. While this may hinder an ambitious employee's advancement, it is indicative of a high level of job satisfaction.

Law enforcement officers may also decide to pursue careers as police officers, detectives, or security experts.

EARNINGS

Salaries for workers in government agencies are based on individuals' level of responsibility and experience. Employees are assigned salary grade levels. As they gain more experience, they are promoted to higher grade levels, or to higher salary steps within their grade levels.

The National Park Service classifies law enforcement professionals under the General Schedule. Most rangers begin at or below the GS-5 level, which in 2009 translated to earning between $27,026 and $31,401. The average ranger in 2009 was on the second step of the GS-7 level, which translates to a salary of $34,953. The most experienced rangers can earn $43,521, which is the highest salary step in the GS-7 level. To move beyond this level, most rangers must become supervisors, subdistrict rangers, district rangers, or division chiefs. At these higher levels, people can earn more than $89,000 per year. These positions are difficult to obtain, however, because the turnover rate for positions above the GS-7 level is exceptionally low.

According to Payscale.com, in 2010 rangers employed by state parks earned annual salaries ranging from $24,144 to $45,909.

Security guards employed by local governments earned mean annual salaries of $32,370 in 2009, according to the U.S. Department of Labor.

Cultural resources law enforcement officers receive benefits such as paid vacations, sick leave, paid holidays, health and life insurance, and pension plans. Some federal agencies provide housing to employees who work in remote areas.

WORK ENVIRONMENT

Law enforcement officers spend the majority of their time patrolling the vast expanses of our nation's public lands. They work in all types of weather conditions. They must be in excellent shape in order to hike to remote areas, although they sometimes conduct patrols on horseback or by using boats and motorized vehicles. Law enforcement officers work day and night to protect cultural resources. This requires them to occasionally be away from family during holidays and weekends. Some officers may also guard resources thar are on display at museums and park visitor centers. In these settings, officers have more traditional hours, although some night-duty may be required.

A career as a cultural resources law enforcement officer can sometimes be dangerous—especially when they encounter and seek to apprehend looters in remote areas. Officers are well-trained to handle these situations, and many report high career satisfation despite the occasional dangers and demands of the job.

OUTLOOK

Employment opportunities at state and local parks should be only fair in coming years. Some states or communities have closed parks due to budget cuts, and turnover in top positions is typically low.

Despite overseeing hundreds of millions of acres, federal agencies that manage and protect cultural and natural resources do not employ a large number of law enforcement officers. Because these agencies are small, job opportunities are limited and, although they are not highly lucrative, they are considered very attractive to individuals who have a desire to protect archaeological resources. Consequently, competition for jobs is very intense. This is not a situation that is likely to improve, since turnover rates are low and new parks, monuments, national forests, and other protected land holdings are seldom added.

Students who are interested in working as cultural resources law enforcement officers should not be discouraged, however. Determined people will always be able to land a job if they really want to; they just have to be willing to take a seasonal or entry-level position and be willing to relocate to where there is an opening.

FOR MORE INFORMATION

For information on careers, education, and training for museum professionals, contact
American Association of Museums
1575 Eye Street, NW, Suite 400
Washington, DC 20005-1113
Tel: 202-289-1818
http://www.aam-us.org

Visit the BLM Web site for information on its land holdings and career and volunteer opportunities.
Bureau of Land Management (BLM)
U.S. Department of the Interior
1849 C Street, NW, Room 5665
Washington, DC 20240-0001
Tel: 202-208-3801
http://www.blm.gov

Visit the NPS Web site for information on national parks and other protected areas in the United States, careers, and volunteer opportunities, internships, and youth programs.
National Park Service (NPS)
U.S. Department of the Interior
1849 C Street, NW
Washington, DC 20240-0001
202-208-3818
http://www.nps.gov

For career and educational opportunities in historic preservation, information on advocacy groups and forums, internship possibilities, and to obtain a copy of its bimonthly magazine, Preservation, *contact*
National Trust for Historic Preservation
1785 Massachusetts Avenue, NW
Washington, DC 20036-2117
Tel: 202-588-6000
http://www.preservationnation.org

The U.S. Fish and Wildlife Service manages the 96-million-acre National Wildlife Refuge System. This system includes 548 National Wildlife Refuges, thousands of smaller wetlands, and other special management areas. Visit its Web site for information on careers, conservation, endangered species, and volunteer opportunities.

U.S. Fish and Wildlife Service
U.S. Department of the Interior
Division of Human Resources
4401 North Fairfax Drive, MS 330
Arlington, VA 22203-1610
Tel: 703-358-1780
http://www.fws.gov/jobs/wwd_law.html

For information about careers and information on national forests, contact

U.S. Forest Service
U.S. Department of Agriculture
Law Enforcement and Investigations
1621 North Kent Street, Suite 1015 RPE
Arlington, VA 22209-2126
Tel: 703-605-4690
E-mail: usfslei@fs.fed.us
http://www.fs.fed.us/lei
http://www.fs.fed.us/fsjobs/jobs_overview.shtml

Cultural Resources Lawyers

OVERVIEW

Lawyers who specialize in cultural resources law work to protect our nation's cultural resources—archaeological sites and objects, prehistoric and historic structures, cultural landscapes, and any other physical evidence of past human cultures. *Cultural resources lawyers,* who are also known as *cultural resources attorneys,* work for government agencies and private organizations and individuals.

HISTORY

The United States has a wealth of culture resources—ranging from Native American archaeological sites, to battlefields, to historic towns and buildings. These resources largely went unprotected until the early 1900s. Many sites were looted, destroyed during construction, or otherwise damaged before archaeological studies and conservation could be conducted.

It was not until the passage of the Antiquities Act in 1906 by Congress that federally owned cultural resources began receiving strong protection. The act, according to the National Park Service, "decreed presidential authority to establish National Monuments and required permits to be approved before archaeological investigations could be undertaken on federal land." The Antiquities Act, combined with the passage of the Historic Sites Act of 1935, helped to launch an era in which more archaeological sites and other cultural resources were protected. People became more educated about the importance of protecting cultural resources and began seeking legal means to ensure their preservation. During the following decades, many other laws were passed to protect cultural resources.

In 1966, the National Historic Preservation Act mandated that the federal government should "provide leadership" for preservation, "contribute to" and "give maximum encouragement" to preservation, and "foster conditions under which our modern society and our prehistoric and historic resources can exist in productive harmony." Over the years, several important laws have been enacted to further protect archaeological and cultural resources, including the Archaeological Resources Protection Act (1979) and the Native American Graves Protection and Repatriation Act (1990).

The passage of these and other laws (including those passed at local and state levels) has created a growing demand for law professionals with specialized knowledge of cultural resources. Cultural resources lawyers serve as key advocates for our nation's cultural heritage.

THE JOB

Cultural resources law is a diverse field with many practice areas. Cultural resources (CR) lawyers are employed by government agencies at all levels, tribal governments, and private organizations to ensure that cultural property is legally protected. The following paragraphs provide an overview of typical work settings and job duties for CR lawyers.

Many CR lawyers are employed by advocacy organizations such as the National Trust for Historic Preservation. One of their main duties is to ensure that cultural resources are protected. They meet with state and federal officials as part of the legal process required by Section 106 of the National Historic Preservation Act when projects are being initiated that may affect a cultural resource such as a Civil War battlefield; prehistoric Native American village, petroglyph site, or burial mound; or other historic site. They may also write and send formal comments to federal agencies regarding these projects. If an advocacy organization deems that a construction or land-use project will damage a cultural resource, it might determine that legal action is necessary to protect the resource. In this instance, lawyers would file a lawsuit against the organization or agency to stop the project from continuing. For example, the National Trust for Historic Preservation, a local preservation organization, and concerned residents recently filed a lawsuit to challenge a local government's approval of construction of a Wal-Mart store within the historic boundaries of Wilderness Battlefield, a major Civil War battlefield in Virginia. In this instance, CR lawyers drafted briefs, motions, and other legal documents and represented the trust during court proceedings. Lawyers would also represent the trust if the organization that was being sued sought to reach a settlement.

CR lawyers also work in the criminal justice system. *Prosecutors* conduct criminal and civil proceedings on behalf of the government. They have a variety of job titles based on what level of government they are employed by and their responsibilities. At the city level, prosecutors are often known as *assistant city attorneys* and *city attorneys*. Prosecutors who work at the county level are known as *assistant district attorneys, assistant prosecuting attorneys, prosecuting attorneys,* and *district attorneys.* At the state level, prosecutors are known as *assistant state attorneys* and *state's attorneys.* Federal prosecutors are known as *assistant U.S. attorneys* or *U.S. attorneys.* Some prosecutors are elected (for example, district attorneys) and others (such as U.S. attorneys) are appointed by government officials.

Prosecutors are involved in a variety of cultural resources-related cases. For example, one major case in the American Southwest involved the theft and trafficking of archaeological objects (prayer sticks, sandals, burial objects, and ceramic bowls and jars) from Native American sites in Colorado, New Mexico, and Utah. Twenty-five people were charged with multiple counts of violating the Native American Graves Protection and Repatriation Act (NAGPRA) and the Archaeological Resources Protection Act. Another case involved the theft of buttons, rifle shells, and belt buckles from a Civil War battlefield, along with the disturbance of human remains and physical damage to the battlefield.

Prosecutors in cases such as these gather and analyze evidence and review laws and legal materials relevant to the case. At the defendant's first court appearance, known as a first appearance, the prosecutor states the charges (for example, stealing antiquities protected under NAGPRA) and recommends the bail amount. Prosecutors may also recommend that some defendants be denied bail if they are considered a danger to the public or a flight risk. The next step in states that do not use a grand jury to indict is the preliminary hearing, in which the prosecutor presents evidence (such as examples of the stolen items found in the possession of the defendant [Native American funerary objects, weapons illegally excavated from a battlefield, etc.] or video of the crime being committed) that helps the judge determine if probable cause exists and whether the defendant charged is the person who committed the crime. After this, an arraignment is scheduled. The prosecutor meets with the defendant and his or her attorneys to discuss the charges. He or she presents all evidence and charges against the defendant. At this time, a plea bargain—the act of a defendant being charged for the lesser of multiple crimes in exchange for an admission of guilt—may be discussed. Most criminal prosecutions in the United States, about 90 percent, are resolved through some form of plea bargain. Sometimes, defendants refuse to plead guilty, or the alleged crime is too serious to strike a plea bargain. In such cases prosecutors are challenged to prove "beyond a reasonable doubt" the defendant is guilty of the crime. Prosecutors often must appear before a judge numerous times to defend the validity of the charge or challenge special requests from the defense (such as moving the case to another location)—even before the case is officially brought to trial. Once at trial, prosecutors begin by making an opening statement that provides the judge or jury an official account of the alleged crime. They present evidence, call witnesses or specialists to give testimony (including citizens or cultural resources law enforcement officers who witnessed the crime), and cross examine witnesses and challenge any evidence presented by the defense. If the defendant is convicted, the judge decides on the severity of the sentence, though prosecutors may make a recommendation.

Defense lawyers represent people who have been accused of breaking cultural resources protection laws. They interview clients and witnesses to ascertain facts in a case, correlate their findings with known cases, and prepare a case to defend a client against the charges made. They conduct a defense at the trial, examine witnesses, and summarize the case with a closing argument to a jury.

Museums and cultural centers employ cultural resources lawyers to help them comply with cultural resources laws such as NAGPRA. These lawyers represent the museum in negotiations with Native American tribes that are seeking repatriation of human remains and funerary objects that are in the museum's collection. In most instances, lawyers arrange a settlement with the tribe and items are returned. If the museum believes that the items in question are not covered under NAGPRA or other cultural resources protection laws, it will ask the lawyer to contest the claims and, if necessary, represent its interests in court. Lawyers also may represent museums that have been accused of having holdings that were obtained illegally during wartime or other times of strife—for example, items that allegedly were looted from a museum by an occupying army during World War II.

CR lawyers may work in private practice—providing advice about Section 106 of the National Historic Preservation Act and other

Books to Read

Forsyth, Marion P. *Presenting Archaeology in Court: A Guide to Legal Protection of Sites.* Lanham, Md.: AltaMira Press, 2006.
Hutt, Sherry. *Cultural Property Law: A Practitioner's Guide to the Management, Protection, and Preservation of Heritage Resources.* Chicago: American Bar Association, 2004.
King, Thomas F. *Cultural Resource Laws and Practice.* 3d ed. Lanham, Md.: AltaMira Press, 2008.
Richman, Jennifer R., and Marion P. Forsyth. *Legal Perspectives on Cultural Resources.* Lanham, Md.: AltaMira Press, 2004.

federal preservation laws to lawyers and others from conservation groups, archaeology organizations, and Native American tribes. Other lawyers may provide advice to landowners about cultural resources-related issues and represent them in legal proceedings. For instance, they may help a private landowner create a preservation easement that permanently protects their property (an archaeological site, a Revolutionary War battlefield, a historic home or other structure, etc.) from development. As mentioned earlier, private practice CR lawyers represent clients who have been accused of violating cultural resources laws. Some CR lawyers teach at colleges and universities. Others become media experts and write books and scholarly articles about cultural resources law and issues in the field.

REQUIREMENTS

High School

A high school diploma, a college degree, and three years of law school are minimum requirements for a law degree. A high school diploma is a first step on the ladder of education that a lawyer must climb. If you are considering a career in law, courses such as government, history, social studies, and economics provide a solid background for entering college-level courses. Speech courses are also helpful to build strong communication skills necessary for the profession. Also take advantage of any computer-related classes or experience you can get, because lawyers often use technology to research and interpret the law, from surfing the Internet to searching legal databases. If you want to work in cultural resources law, it is a good idea to take history and geography courses, as well as any anthropology and archaeology classes.

Postsecondary Training

To enter any law school approved by the American Bar Association (ABA), you must satisfactorily complete at least three, and usually four, years of college work. Most law schools do not specify any particular courses for prelaw education. Usually a liberal arts track is most advisable, with courses in English, history, economics, social sciences, logic, and public speaking. A college student planning on specialization in a particular area of law, however, might also take courses significantly related to that area; for example, they should take history, archaeology, anthropology, geography, and other related classes if they plan to pursue a career in cultural resources law.

Currently, 200 law schools in the United States are approved by the ABA; others, many of them night schools, are approved by state authorities only. Most of the approved law schools, however, do have night sessions to accommodate part-time students. Part-time courses of study usually take four years.

Law school training consists of required courses such as legal writing and research, contracts, criminal law, constitutional law, torts, and property. The second and third years may be devoted to specialized courses of interest to the student, such as evidence, business transactions and corporations, or admiralty. The study of cases and decisions is of basic importance to the law student, who will be required to read and study thousands of these cases. A degree of juris doctor (J.D.) or bachelor of laws (LL.B.) is usually granted upon graduation.

Some law schools offer courses or programs that focus on cultural resources law. Contact the ABA for a list of programs.

College training in anthropology or archaeology is not required, but will provide an excellent background for people interested in working in this field.

Some federal agencies, such as the National Park Service, offer training programs and seminars about cultural resources law to practicing federal and tribal attorneys.

Certification or Licensing

Every state requires that lawyers be admitted to the bar of that state before they can practice. They require that applicants graduate from an approved law school and that they pass a written examination in the state in which they intend to practice. In a few states, graduates of law schools within the state are excused from these written examinations. After lawyers have been admitted to the bar in one state, they can practice in another state without taking a written examination if the states have reciprocity agreements; however, they will be required to meet certain state standards of good character and legal experience and pay any applicable fees.

Other Requirements

Federal courts and agencies have their own rules regulating admission to practice. Other requirements vary among the states.

Lawyers have to be effective communicators, work well with people, be attentive to detail and highly organized, and be able to find creative solutions to problems, such as complex court cases.

EXPLORING

If you think a career as a lawyer might be right up your alley, there are several ways you can find out more about it before making that final decision. Ask your school counselor to arrange a telephone or in-person information interview with a CR lawyer. If you are unable to interview a CR attorney, talking with a lawyer in general practice will provide you with a general overview of what it is like to be a lawyer. Ask questions and get the scoop on what the field is all about. Also, talk to your counselor or political science teacher about starting or joining a job-shadowing program. Job-shadowing programs allow you to follow a person in a certain career around for a day or two to get an idea of what goes on in a typical day. You may even be invited to help out with a few minor duties.

You can also search the Internet for information about cultural resources law and past and current court cases. Read books about cultural resources law to obtain a general overview of the field (see "Books to Read" for a short list).

If you are already in law school, you might consider becoming a student member of the American Bar Association. Student members receive *Student Lawyer,* a magazine that contains useful information for aspiring lawyers. Sample articles from the magazine can be read at http://www.abanet.org/lsd/studentlawyer.

EMPLOYERS

Cultural resources lawyers are employed by government agencies at all levels such as the National Park Service, Bureau of Land Management, the Advisory Council on Historic Preservation, and state and local historical preservation offices. They work for private advocacy organizations, such as the National Trust for Historic Preservation, and tribal governments. Some CR lawyers work in private practice.

Many professionals work part time in cultural resources law while practicing in other areas such as environmental law.

STARTING OUT

The first steps in entering the law profession are graduation from an approved law school and passing a state bar examination. Usually beginning lawyers do not go into solo practice right away. It is often difficult to become established, and additional experience is helpful to the beginning lawyer. Also, most lawyers do not specialize in cultural resources law without first gaining experience. Beginning lawyers usually work as assistants to experienced lawyers. At first they do mainly research and routine work. After a few years of successful experience, they may be ready to go out on their own. Other choices open to the beginning lawyer include joining an established law firm or entering into partnership with another lawyer.

New lawyers employed by government agencies start out as junior members of a legal department and gradually gain experience and responsibilities. Those involved in cultural resources law gradually gain an understanding of the field and experience working as a member of a legal team on cases.

Many new lawyers are recruited by law firms or other employers directly from law school. Recruiters come to the school and interview possible hires. Other new graduates can get job leads from local and state bar associations. Direct application to organizations, such as the National Trust for Historic Preservation or state historic preservation offices, that deal with cultural resources issues is highly recommended.

ADVANCEMENT

Lawyers with outstanding ability can expect to go a long way in their profession. Novice lawyers generally start as law clerks, but as they prove themselves and develop their abilities, many opportunities for advancement will arise. They may be promoted to junior partner in a law firm, become district attorneys, lead lawyers on high-profile government cases, or establish their own practice. Lawyers may enter politics and become judges, mayors, congressmen, or other government leaders. Top positions are available in business, too, for the qualified lawyer. Lawyers working for the federal government advance according to the civil service system.

EARNINGS

There is no specific salary information available for lawyers employed in cultural resources law. The U.S. Department of Labor does provide information on salaries for all lawyers. It reports that the 2009 median salary for practicing lawyers was $113,240. Ten percent earned less than $55,270 and 10 percent earned more than $166,400. General attorneys in the federal government received $127,550 in 2009. State and local government attorneys generally made less, earning $82,750 and $91,040, respectively, in 2009. Some lawyers at private firms can earn more than $300,000 annually.

According to the *2008 Public Sector and Public Interest Attorney Salary Report,* from the National Association for Law Placement, entry-level prosecutors at the local level earned median annual salaries of $45,675. Those employed for five years earned $60,000, while those with 11–15 years on the job made $77,500. The association reports the following median salaries for state prosecuting attorneys in 2008 by level of experience: entry-level, $50,000; five years, $62,780; and 11–15 years, $80,830.

The U.S. Attorney's Offices use an Administratively Determined pay schedule, which is based on the amount of experience an individual has and other qualifications. Information on this pay schedule is unavailable, but prosecuting attorneys at the federal level typically earn salaries that are equivalent to the GS-11 to GS-15 categories on the General Schedule scale (another pay scale that is used for government workers). In 2009, government employees at these levels earned base salaries that ranged from $49,544 to $127,604.

Benefits include paid vacation, health, disability, life insurance, and retirement or pension plans. Some employers also offer profit-sharing plans.

WORK ENVIRONMENT

Offices and courtrooms are usually pleasant, although busy, places to work. Lawyers also spend significant amounts of time in law libraries or record rooms, in the homes and offices of clients, and sometimes in the jail cells of clients or prospective witnesses. CR lawyers often visit the areas they are tasked with protecting—such as a Civil War battlefield in rural Virginia, a Native American petroglyph site in the mountains of Wyoming, an archaeological site on a Native American reservation, or an African-American slave cemetery found at a construction site in a bustling city. Many lawyers never work in a courtroom. Unless they are directly involved in litigation, they may never perform at a trial.

Court hours for most lawyers are usually regular business hours, with a one-hour lunch break. Often lawyers have to work long hours, spending evenings and weekends preparing cases and materials and working with clients. In addition to the work, the lawyer must always keep up with the latest developments in the profession and their specialty (such as new cultural resources protection laws passed by Congress or the status of current court cases). Also, it takes a long time to become a qualified lawyer, and it may be difficult to earn an adequate living until the lawyer gets enough experience to develop an established private practice.

Lawyers who are employed at law firms must often work grueling hours to advance in the firm. Spending long weekend hours doing research, interviewing people, and traveling to archaeological sites and other protected areas should be expected.

OUTLOOK

According to the *Occupational Outlook Handbook,* employment for lawyers employed in all industry sectors is expected to grow about as fast as the average for all occupations through 2018, but large numbers of law school graduates have created strong competition for jobs, even though the number of graduates has begun to level off. Opportunities for cultural resources lawyers should be good, but it is important to remember that this field is relatively small and it takes years of experience to build a successful private practice or obtain top positions with government agencies or historic preservation organizations. Many attorneys practice cultural resources law part time while also practicing general law or specializing in a related field.

FOR MORE INFORMATION

For information about careers in law, contact
American Bar Association
Section of Environment, Energy, and Resources
321 North Clark Street
Chicago, IL 60654-7598
Tel: 800-285-2221
E-mail: askaba@abanet.org
http://www.abanet.org
http://www.abanet.org/environ

For information on workshops and seminars, contact
Association of American Law Schools
1201 Connecticut Avenue, NW, Suite 800

Washington, DC 20036-2717
Tel: 202-296-8851
E-mail: aals@aals.org
http://www.aals.org

The FBA provides information for lawyers and judges involved in federal practice.
Federal Bar Association (FBA)
1220 North Fillmore Street, Suite 440
Arlington, VA 22201-6501
Tel: 571-481-9100
E-mail: fba@fedbar.org
http://fedbar.org

For information on choosing a law school, law careers, salaries, and alternative law careers, contact
National Association for Law Placement
1025 Connecticut Avenue, NW, Suite 1110
Washington, DC 20036-5413
Tel: 202-835-1001
E-mail: info@nalp.org
http://www.nalp.org

This is the oldest and largest professional association for prosecutors in the world. Visit its Web site for general information about the field.
National District Attorneys Association
44 Canal Center Plaza, Suite 110
Alexandria, VA 22314-1548
Tel: 703-549-9222
http://www.ndaa.org

For information on archaeological careers and job listings, contact
Society for American Archaeology
900 Second Street, NE, Suite 12
Washington, DC 20002-3560
Tel: 202-789-8200
E-mail: headquarters@saa.org
http://www.saa.org

For career information, contact
Society for Historical Archaeology
9707 Key West Avenue, Suite 100
Rockville, MD 20850-3992

Tel: 301-990-2454
E-mail: hq@sha.org
http://www.sha.org
http://www.sha.org/EHA/splash.cfm

INTERVIEW

Alexander "Ti" Hays V is the public lands counsel with the National Trust for Historic Preservation in Denver, Colorado. He discussed his career with the editors of Careers in Focus: Archaeology.

Q. What is one thing that people may not know about cultural resources law?

A. I think most people would probably be surprised to learn that the legal protections for cultural resources in the United States are not nearly as strong as they are in other countries. For instance, in many other countries, cultural resources—whether located on private or public lands—are owned by the federal government, which often enacts strict laws designed to protect those resources from damage and destruction and prohibiting their removal. However, in the United States, cultural resources on private lands—no matter how significant or rare—are almost always owned by the landowner. Consequently, landowners are usually allowed to damage, destroy, or remove any cultural resources located on their property.

As for cultural resources located on the public lands—that is, lands owned by the U.S. government—Congress has enacted a variety of protective laws, including the National Historic Preservation Act (NHPA) of 1966. The NHPA requires each federal agency to "take into account" the effects of its actions on cultural resources prior to approving or dispersing funds for a project. Yet, although the NHPA is the most comprehensive federal preservation statute in the United States, it does not require federal agencies to actually do anything to protect cultural resources from a project's adverse effects. Thus, even when cultural resources are under federal ownership, they frequently lack the mandatory legal protections that exist in other countries.

Q. Please describe a day in your life on the job. What are your typical work responsibilities? What is your work environment like?

A. As one of only a handful of attorneys in the United States who advocates full time for the protection of cultural resources on the public lands, my responsibilities are wide-ranging. On any given day I may be drafting written comments to a federal agency concerning the effects of a proposed project on cultural resources. Or I may be meeting with federal and state officials, archaeologists, and Native American tribes as part of the consultation process required by Section 106 of the NHPA for federal actions with the potential to affect cultural resources.

Although we strive to resolve our concerns at the administrative level—through written comments and in consultation meetings, we are sometimes forced to file lawsuits and seek relief from the courts. When this occurs, my duties include drafting motions, briefs, and other court documents and representing the National Trust for Historic Preservation during court hearings. I also represent the National Trust during settlement negotiations that sometimes take place with opposing parties.

Besides these formal responsibilities, I am frequently asked to speak on the protection of cultural resources at conferences or before students enrolled in preservation law courses. Additionally, as one of the few attorneys practicing in my area, I am regularly consulted by attorneys and advocates from conservation groups, Native American tribes, and archaeological organizations about Section 106 of the NHPA and other federal preservation laws.

Q. What are the most important personal and professional qualities for cultural resources lawyers?

A. Cultural resources lawyers should possess the same personal qualities that make any attorney an effective advocate. Those qualities include excellent communication skills—both oral and written; close attention to detail; strong organizational skills; and willingness to advocate zealously for positions that may be highly unpopular with other interested parties.

In terms of professional qualifications, cultural resources lawyers do not necessarily need formal training in archaeology or anthropology, although a background in one or both of those disciplines certainly helps. But a cultural resources lawyer should have close familiarity with the federal laws governing the management and protection of cultural resources—the NHPA, National Environmental Policy Act, Antiquities Act of 1906, and Archaeological Resources Protection Act, among others. Several colleges throughout the country offer graduate-level training in these laws, as well as in state and local laws, regulations, and ordinances, and students interested in pursuing a career as a cultural resources lawyer should consider applying to law schools that offer those courses.

Q. What are some of the pros and cons of your job?

A. One of my favorite parts of my job is getting out of the office and into the field to visit the cultural resources for which I advocate. From an advocacy standpoint, this can be an extremely important exercise, because a photograph or written description rarely conveys the setting of a cultural resource, which often contributes so greatly to the significance of a resource, especially when located on public lands. I firmly believe that I am a more effective advocate for Chaco Canyon, for example, because I have walked among the ancient pueblo sites located there and seen firsthand the vast and largely undeveloped setting surrounding the ruins.

Another great part of my job is the work I do with Native American tribes. Because the tribes once inhabited much of the area now within the United States, many of the cultural resources on the public lands—rock art, pueblos, and teepee rings are among the more plentiful—were crafted by their ancestors. In fact, because so many tribes lack written histories, tribes tell and preserve their stories through the cultural resources on the public lands. The small role I play in helping them maintain the fabric of those stories is extremely gratifying.

On the downside, my job does sometimes involve disappointing outcomes. Because federal agencies are required by law to manage much of the public lands for "multiple-uses," including cattle grazing, oil and gas development, and recreation, cultural resources protection can—and often does—get lost in the shuffle when agencies develop plans and weigh project proposals. And because Section 106 of the NHPA provides the agencies with the discretion to approve a project irrespective of any adverse effects on cultural resources, we are sometimes forced to accept the loss of a particular resource's or set of resources' integrity.

Q. What is the employment outlook for cultural resources lawyers?

A. That really depends on the type of job sought by an aspiring cultural resources lawyer. Right now, the prospects are probably a little bit better at the local level, because there are simply more organizations and agencies involved in the protection of cultural resources at that level. Whereas at the national level, the prospects are probably not quite as good, largely because there are so very few national organizations devoted to cultural resources protection. Employment with a Native American tribe is another potential avenue for cultural resources lawyers. However, tribal attorneys normally practice in a wide variety of areas, only one of which is cultural resources law. Law firms represent yet another possibility for cultural resources lawyers, particularly those with no or limited experience, because they will frequently provide pro bono representation to cultural resources advocacy organizations that could not otherwise afford to retain legal counsel.

Q. What has been one of your most rewarding experiences in your career and why?

A. One of the most rewarding experiences of my career involved the listing of New Mexico's Mount Taylor on the state's register of cultural properties. For hundreds of years, pueblos and tribes throughout Arizona and New Mexico have believed Mount Taylor to be a sacred place. To this day, pueblo and tribal members make pilgrimages to the mountain to conduct religious ceremonies, visit shrines, and gather plants for traditional ceremonies.

Yet, in spite of Mount Taylor's significance to the nearby pueblos and tribes, state agencies were not consulting with them prior to authorizing potentially destructive activities on the mountain. For this reason, the pueblos of Acoma, Laguna, and Zuni, Hopi Tribe, and Navajo Nation chose to nominate the mountain to the state register, as state agencies must consult with tribal groups over projects that may affect cultural properties listed in the register. Although I played a secondary, supporting role to the tribes in this effort—drafting letters of support to state officials and review boards, attending public hearings, and helping secure media coverage for the nomination—it was an extremely rewarding moment when the state, over the intense objections of industry groups, decided to approve the nomination and list Mount Taylor in the state register.

Cultural Resources Management Archaeologists and Managers

OVERVIEW

Cultural resources can be defined as important archaeological sites and objects, prehistoric and historic structures, cultural landscapes, and ethnographic resources. *Cultural resources management archaeologists and managers* determine if cultural resources are present at proposed construction and land use sites (such as buildings, roads, bridges, highways, and dams) and document and/or recover these resources before the project begins. Some sites have also been discovered during reconstruction or renovation of existing structures. When working with larger projects, CRM often turn to the services of *contract archaeologists* to survey and evaluate potential sites.

HISTORY

Cultural resources management (CRM) emerged in the late 1960s as a result of the passage of three laws: the National Historic Preservation Act of 1966, the Department of Transportation Act of 1966, and the National Environmental Policy Act of 1969. These laws required U.S. federal government agencies to consider the archaeological, historical, and cultural impact of any construction or land use projects that were undertaken on federal lands, that were funded by the federal government but on private lands, or that required a permit from the federal government (such as areas where cell towers are constructed). The laws also created administrative bodies run by the National Park Service, the independent Advisory Council on Historic Preservation, and historic preservation offices in every state. In the late 1960s and early 1970s, tribal, state, and local governments also began developing CRM programs. Private CRM consulting firms and other companies emerged to help government agencies and private companies comply with these laws and regulations.

According to *Archaeology Essentials: Theories, Methods, and Practice*, by Colin Renfrew and Paul Bahn, CRM archaeology makes up at least 90 percent of all field archaeology that is conducted in the United States.

In 1995, the American Cultural Resources Association was founded to "support and promote the common interests of for-profit cultural resource management firms of all sizes, types and specialties."

THE JOB

When plans to build a new highway near Phoenix, Arizona, were given the green light, government officials took steps to ensure that the work would be in compliance with state and federal CRM laws. One of their first steps in preparation for the project was to hire a group of CRM archaeologists to survey the site and perform excavations and salvage archaeology, if necessary. Officials from Arizona's State Historic Preservation Office (SHPO) felt there was a good chance the proposed site had archaeological significance due to its proximity to known Native American archaeological sites. Thanks to the expertise of archaeologists from Arizona's SHPO, the work of CRM archaeologists, and the local, state, and federal laws that were in place that protected sites from simply being destroyed amidst construction, valuable archaeological artifacts and data were located and preserved for the appreciation of the public and study by scientists. In this instance, CRM archaeologists uncovered pit houses, pottery, tools, and human remains dating to the Hohokam Classic Period (circa A.D. 1100 to 1450).

Archaeologists conduct the hands-on work that is involved in cultural resources management projects. *Project managers* oversee the entire project. They create a plan of attack for the project; assemble in-house staff and hire temporary support and field staff to do the work; manage the day-to-day operation of the project; oversee budgets and expenditures; serve as the intermediary between clients and project staff; interact with the public (including Native American tribes) that may be affected by the work or have culturally-based objections to the project; and ensure compliance with local, state, federal, and tribal cultural resources law and regulations. Project managers may also be known as *principal investigators* or *lead archaeologists,* although at some firms project managers supervise these workers.

Most CRM projects are broken down into three phases: Phase I: Survey; Phase II: Evaluation/Test Excavation; and Phase III: Salvage Excavation/Data Recovery. Most projects do not reach Phase III since not every site yields culturally significant materials. In some cases, a site is so rich in artifacts and cultural remains that archaeologists may suggest revisions to building plans (such as altering the depth or location of a building site) in order to protect the site. The following paragraphs provide an overview of the three major phases of CRM archaeology.

Phase I: Survey. Archaeologists begin each project by reviewing the proposed plan for the construction or land use project to see if any areas match up with already identified archaeological sites. Experts then travel to the site to further identify potential sites. This is often referred to as a reconnaissance survey; these surveys can be conducted on the ground or with the help of an aircraft or using a camera strapped to a large balloon. A more in-depth survey and excavation may be required to locate additional sites of cultural importance. Archaeologists often conduct a shovel test, a very small excavation, to determine if artifacts, structures, and/or remains are present.

In some instances, no shovel tests are conducted, and CRM archaeologists are hired to monitor the site during construction to ensure that cultural resources are not discovered. If cultural materials are found during construction (for example, pottery shards), the archaeologist may halt the project to determine exactly what has been found. If the materials are deemed not to be culturally significant, the project continues. If culturally important materials are found, the archaeologist creates a plan that protects the materials or orders scientific excavation to document and remove them for further study (see Phase III).

Phase II: Evaluation/Test Excavation. If a substantial number of artifacts are found, archaeologists may conduct a deeper, more thorough excavation. These tests are done to determine if significant collections of artifacts (called cultural deposits) are present. These materials are then sent to a laboratory for analysis. For example, excavation may discover that the potsherds discovered in Phase I fieldwork were the only materials present at the site, and were most

A cultural resources management archaeologist (*left*) and a museum director sort artifacts. (*Terry Ketron, AP Photo*/The Daily Sun)

likely left by a nomadic tribe. In this instance, the potsherds are cataloged and stored for further research, and the construction project can begin. On the other hand, if further excavation and laboratory study reveals more substantial finds (entire pots, fire pits, garbage pits, and remains of bones, weapons, and even ancient humans), the archaeologist puts the construction project on hold and the inquiry moves to Phase III.

Phase III: Salvage Excavation/Data Recovery. Phase III work occurs when culturally significant sites are found. Examples of such sites would include a prehistoric burial mound from the Mississippian Native American culture discovered during the construction of an army base; a Civil War battle site found at a residential construction site just outside the boundaries of Kennesaw Mountain National Battlefield Park in Georgia; or the remains of a colonial-era street discovered during highway construction.

Unfortunately, some culturally significant sites must be destroyed to accommodate new roads, bridges, airports, highways, or dams. In such cases, archaeologists conduct a large-scale excavation, known as salvage excavation or data recovery, in which they collect as much data as possible before the site is destroyed. For example, the rebuilding of major highways in Connecticut left 18th-century homesteads in jeopardy. Archaeologists conducted a complete excavation of the sites, uncovering structural walls of several houses and everyday items including glass bottles and ceramic cookware that told the story of the occupants. Each item recovered was meticulously analyzed and conserved, and the information provided insight into 18th-century colonial life.

In addition to conducting fieldwork, CRM archaeologists study and conserve recovered artifacts for future display in museums. They spend a considerable amount of time writing reports for government agencies. They may also catalog items for inclusion in digital databases that make CRM projects more accessible to academics and the general public. Some CRM archaeologists write papers or reports documenting their finds for professional trade journals (although this is less common in the specialty of CRM archaeology). Others teach students about CRM archaeology at colleges and universities.

Interesting Web Sites

About.com: Archaeology
http://archaeology.about.com

Archaeological Parks in the U.S.
http://www.uark.edu/misc/aras

The Archaeology Channel
http://www.archaeologychannel.org

Bureau of Land Management: Adventures in the Past
http://www.blm.gov/heritage/adventures/vacation.html

Frequently Asked Questions About a Career in Archaeology in the U.S.
http://www.museum.state.il.us/ismdepts/anthro/dlcfaq.html

National Park Service: Archaeology for Kids
http://www.nps.gov/archeology/public/kids/index.htm

National Park Service: Archaeology Program
http://www.nps.gov/archeology

Passport in Time
http://www.passportintime.com

REQUIREMENTS

High School

Take a college preparatory program in high school that includes courses in history, mathematics, computer science, social studies, and science. English and speech courses will help you develop your communication skills. You should also take Spanish, which will come in handy when you work in areas where a large percentage of Spanish-speaking people live. Other foreign languages will also be helpful, depending on where you find employment. For example, many archaeologists conduct research at sites that were inhabited by explorers or settlers from non-English-speaking lands such as Russia, Portugal, and France.

Postsecondary Training

The minimum educational requirement for cultural resources archaeologists and managers is a bachelor's degree in archaeology, anthropology, or a closely related discipline. Many CRM employers require that job candidates have a master's degree. Government agencies and organizations that adhere to the U.S. Secretary of the Interior's Professional Qualifications Standards require archaeologists and managers to have at least a master's degree. Additionally, you will need a master's degree or doctorate to teach at colleges and universities.

Archaeology departments are typically part of anthropology departments; few separate archaeology departments exist in U.S. colleges and universities. Some colleges and universities offer bachelor's and graduate degrees in cultural resources management, while others offer concentrations or minors. Typical required classes in a CRM degree program include CRM I and II, Archaeology Seminar, Technical Writing, and Biology Anthropology or Cultural Anthropology. Elective courses might include Lab Methods in Archaeology, Field Methods in Anthropology, Contemporary American Indian Issues, Techniques in Geographic Information Systems, Geomorphology, Introduction to Public History, Essentials of Forensic Anthropology and Archaeology, and Introduction to Graduate Statistics.

Certification or Licensing

The Register of Professional Archaeologists offers voluntary registration to archaeologists who agree to "abide by an explicit code of conduct and standards of research performance; who hold a graduate degree in archaeology, anthropology, art history, classics, history, or another germane discipline; and who have substantial practical experience." An increasing number of CRM firms require that their employees receive registration from the Register of Professional Archaeologists.

Other Requirements

Successful cultural resources archaeologists and managers have excellent communication and organizational skills. They have analytical minds and enjoy solving problems and conducting research. They are good time managers and are able to work effectively under deadline pressure. They also have good interpersonal skills, but can work on their own if required. Archaeologists and managers should be very knowledgeable about laws that relate to cultural resources management and be willing to continue to learn throughout their careers.

EXPLORING

Participating in an archaeological dig during your summer vacation will provide you with an excellent introduction to the field. Many colleges, universities, and professional archaeology associations organize such programs.

Reading books about cultural resources management and archaeology is another good way to learn about the field. Here are a few suggestions: *Archaeology For Dummies,* by Nancy Marie White (Hoboken, N.J.: For Dummies, 2008); *Practicing Archaeology: An Introduction to Cultural Resources Archaeology,* 2d edition, by Thomas W. Neumann (Lanham, Md.: AltaMira Press, 2009); and *Doing Archaeology: A Cultural Resource Management Perspective,* by Thomas F. King (Walnut Creek, Calif.: Left Coast Press Inc., 2005). Periodicals such *American Archaeology* (http://www.americanarchaeology.com/aamagazine.html) and *Archaeology* (http://www.archaeology.org) will provide you with a general overview of the field. Additionally, the National Park Service published *Cultural Resource Management* until 2002. Past issues can be accessed at http://www.nps.gov/history/crm.

Check out Web sites, too. One suggestion: the National Park Service's Archaeology Program Web site, http://www.nps.gov/archeology.

The U.S. Forest Service offers Passport in Time, a "volunteer archaeology and historic preservation program . . . where volunteers work with professional Forest Service archaeologists and historians on national forests throughout the U.S. on such diverse activities as archaeological survey and excavation, rock art restoration, survey, archival research, historic structure restoration, oral history gathering, and analysis and curation of artifacts." Visit http://www.passportintime.com for more information.

EMPLOYERS

Most cultural resources management archaeologists and managers are employed in the private sector by CRM firms or large companies that provide engineering, environmental impact, or planning services. The American Cultural Resources Association estimates that there are approximately 1,600 to 1,800 CRM firms in the United States. Other employers include colleges and universities, nonprofit organizations, tribal governments, museums, federal agencies (National Park Service, U.S. Forest Service, Bureau of Land Management, Bureau of Indian Affairs, Natural Resources Conservation Service, etc.), and state and municipal agencies (highway, parks, and environment departments). The CRM administrative bodies run by the National Park Service, the independent Advisory Council on Historic Preservation, and each state's historic preservation office also employ CRM archaeologists and managers. Some CRM professionals are self-employed and run their own consulting firms.

STARTING OUT

Your college's career services office will be able to provide a list of CRM employers and job opportunities. You can also learn about possible employment options during college and postgraduate internships, fellowships, and fieldwork experiences.

The American Cultural Resources Association offers a list of member firms at its Web site, http://www.acra-crm.org. These companies provide a wealth of job opportunities to archaeologists and managers.

Many archaeology professional associations and organizations offer job listings at their Web sites. Archaeology-oriented employment sites that provide job listings include Earthworks-jobs.com (http://www.earthworks-jobs.com), eCulturalResources (http://www.eculturalresources.com/jobs.php), and ArchaeologyFieldwork.com (http://www.archaeologyfieldwork.com).

ADVANCEMENT

Cultural resources management archaeologists and managers advance by receiving pay raises, being asked to work on larger projects, seeking employment at larger CRM firms, leaving the field to work as professors, writing books about their work, and starting their own CRM firms. Archaeologists can also advance by transitioning into management positions.

EARNINGS

In 2009, the American Cultural Resources Association conducted a survey of its members to obtain information about salaries. It found that project managers had hourly earnings that ranged from $17 to $58 in 2008, with mean earnings of $28.06. Mean hourly earnings for principal investigators, senior archaeologists, and senior architectural historians were $30.58. Hourly earnings ranged from $16 to $99. Archaeologists, field directors, and project archaeologists earned hourly salaries that ranged from $15 to $65, with a mean of $22.73.

Median annual earnings for all anthropologists and archaeologists were $53,460 in 2009, according to the U.S. Department of Labor. Salaries ranged from less than $31,530 to $87,890 or more.

Some CRM archaeologists work in academia. According to the U.S. Department of Labor, college and university archaeology professors earned between $41,270 and $119,070 in 2009, depending on the type of institution. Median annual earnings were $69,520.

Full-time workers receive a variety of benefits including paid vacation, health insurance, disability, life insurance, and retirement or pension plans. An American Cultural Resources Association member survey found that 69 percent of its members provided health insurance for employees; 63 percent offered retirement and profit-sharing plans; and 79 percent of companies provided reimbursement for employees' professional development.

WORK ENVIRONMENT

Cultural resources management archaeologists and managers work in all types of field settings—from dusty deserts and dam sites near raging rivers, to icy mountaintops and tropical rainforests, to the sides of busy highways, to industrial and residential construction sites in cities and suburbs. They also work in clean, well-lit offices when reviewing site surveys, conducting research, and preparing reports.

A typical workweek in this field is about 40 hours, with overtime necessary when deadlines are pending. Unlike traditional archaeological fieldwork, this is a fast-paced specialty. There is a lot of pressure to complete projects quickly so that construction and land use projects are not delayed.

While all archaeological fieldwork should be conducted using universal scientific standards, CRM archaeology differs from traditional archaeology in that it does not involve long-term research and scholarship. Official reports for government agencies are written and submitted, but then CRM archaeologists and managers move on to the next project. Some archaeologists may not enjoy the fast-paced and transitory nature of CRM archaeology and choose instead to pursue a career in academic or research archaeology.

OUTLOOK

The U.S. Department of Labor predicts that employment for archaeologists will grow much faster than the average for all careers through 2018. Opportunities for cultural resources management archaeologists and managers should be even better. An increasing number of government- and private-funded construction projects has created strong demand for workers in this specialty. It is estimated that cultural resources management archaeology is now a $1 billion industry annually in the United States. Cultural resources management projects make up at least 90 percent of all field archaeology that is conducted. This translates to a massive number of projects and many opportunities for CRM archaeologists and managers. In fact, more than 380,000 CRM projects were conducted in the United States from 1998 to 2003, according to the U.S. Department of the Interior. Look for opportunities to continue to be strong during the next decade and beyond.

FOR MORE INFORMATION

For information on federal CRM laws, training and education programs, and to read related fact sheets and other publications, contact
> **Advisory Council on Historic Preservation**
> 1100 Pennsylvania Avenue, NW, Suite 803
> Washington, DC 20004-2501
> Tel: 202-606-8503
> E-mail: achp@achp.gov
> http://www.achp.gov

For industry information, contact
> **American Cultural Resources Association**
> 5024-R Campbell Boulevard
> Baltimore, MD 21236-5943
> Tel: 410-933-3483
> http://www.acra-crm.org

For an overview of the career of archaeologist written by an associate professor of anthropology, visit
Frequently Asked Questions About a Career in Archaeology in the U.S.
http://www.museum.state.il.us/ismdepts/anthro/dlcfaq.html

For information on state archaeologists and archaeology museums and resources, contact
National Association of State Archaeologists
http://www.uiowa.edu/~osa/nasa

For career and educational opportunities in historic preservation, information on advocacy groups and forums, internship possibilities, and to obtain a copy of its bimonthly magazine, Preservation, *contact*
National Trust for Historic Preservation
1785 Massachusetts Avenue, NW
Washington, DC 20036-2117
Tel: 202-588-6000
http://www.preservationnation.org

For information on professional registration, contact
Register of Professional Archaeologists
5024-R Campbell Boulevard
Baltimore, MD 21236-5943
Tel: 410-933-3486
E-mail: info@rpanet.org
http://www.rpanet.org

For information on archaeology careers and job listings, contact
Society for American Archaeology
900 Second Street, NE, Suite 12
Washington, DC 20002-3560
Tel: 202-789-8200
E-mail: headquarters@saa.org
http://www.saa.org

The SAS is an association for "those interested in advancing our knowledge of the past through a wide range of techniques deriving from the fields of physics, chemistry, and the natural sciences." Visit its Web site for more information.
Society for Archaeological Sciences (SAS)
http://www.socarchsci.org

For career information, contact
Society for Historical Archaeology
9707 Key West Avenue, Suite 100
Rockville, MD 20850-3992
Tel: 301-990-2454
E-mail: hq@sha.org
http://www.sha.org
http://www.sha.org/EHA/splash.cfm

Environmental Archaeologists

OVERVIEW

Environmental archaeologists are specialized archaeologists who study how past cultures interacted with and affected the natural world. Specialists in this field study animals, plants, and landscapes. Environmental archaeologists study ancient materials and modern specimens in order to better understand the relationships between ancient cultures and their environments.

HISTORY

Archaeologists have always taken account of how the environment affected ancient cultures, but it was not until the 1960s that environmental archaeology emerged as a scientific archaeological discipline. In recent years, there has been a growing interest in the study of how ancient cultures interacted with and were affected by their environment. Today, environmental archaeologists are important members of research teams at archaeological digs. They are also being relied on to provide empirical information about climate change.

THE JOB

The field of environmental archaeology is often divided into three subspecialties—*zooarchaeology,* the study of past use of animals by humans; *archaeobotany,* the study of past use of plants by humans; and *geoarchaeology,* the study of nonliving aspects of the

Books to Read

Bahn, Paul, and Colin Renfrew. *Archaeology Essentials: Theories, Methods and Practice.* London, U.K.: Thames & Hudson, 2007.

Bahn, Paul. *The Illustrated World Encyclopedia of Archaeology: A Remarkable Journey Round The World's Major Ancient Sites From The Pyramids Of Giza To Easter Island... Southern France.* London, U.K.: Lorenz Books, 2007.

Cremin, Aedeen. *The World Encyclopedia of Archaeology: The World's Most Significant Sites and Cultural Treasures.* Richmond Hill, O.N. Canada: Firefly Books, 2007.

Darvill, Timothy. *Concise Oxford Dictionary of Archaeology.* 2d ed. New York: Oxford University Press, USA, 2009.

Kelly, Robert L., and David Hurst Thomas. *Archaeology.* 5th ed. Florence, Ky.: Wadsworth Publishing, 2009.

Sutton, Mark Q., and Robert M. Yohe. *Archaeology: The Science of the Human Past.* 3d ed. Columbus, Ohio: Allyn & Bacon, 2007.

White, Nancy Marie. *Archaeology For Dummies.* Hoboken, N.J.: For Dummies, 2008.

landscape such as geology, geography, and weather. Collectively, research conducted in each of these subspecialties can provide a clearer picture of how the environment affected their daily lives and, conversely, how ancient people affected their environment. For example, a cold, harsh climate might have encouraged an ancient culture to pursue a hunter-gatherer lifestyle instead of a sedentary agricultural way of life. Examples of how a culture could affect their environment include overfishing or overgrazing. The following paragraphs provide an overview of each specialty and examples of their work.

Zooarchaeologists try to determine how animals were used by past cultures. For example, zooarchaeologists working at an archaeological site in Western Europe may search for the remains of ancient horses, oxen, and other beasts of burden. If discovered, the bones may prove that a culture that once inhabited the area was advanced enough to use animals as means of transportation or for labor. Zooarchaeologists working at a prehistoric campsite in west Texas may make discoveries regarding bison bones, including the location of bone fragments and larger pieces of bones. They may discover that the prehistoric culture had particular uses for certain bison parts. Some were eaten immediately after the kill, other parts were brought back to camp to consume later or processed for tools or clothing. They may also be able to locate the sites of prehistoric buffalo runs by finding a large number of bones in one concentrated area. (A buffalo run consists of a cliff and the area below it. Prehistoric hunters stampeded herds of buffalo and other animals off these cliffs to their deaths below, then butchered the animals.) Still other zooarchaeologists may determine that certain animals—such as dogs—were kept as pets and not used for labor or food. Another aspect of zooarchaeological research involves the study of carbon isotopes and other elements in the bones of animals through time to measure the degree of environmental change. This research is used to understand climates of ancient times, as well as help assess changes in our current climate. Zooarchaeologists are also called *archaeozoologists*.

Archaeobotanists are interested in how plants were used in the past. They study the preserved remains of plants (including pollen, bark, seeds, spores, nut shells, wood) found at archaeological sites—these plant remains are charred, waterlogged, frozen, desiccated (dried), and even imprinted in clay. Their work not only tells us what ancient peoples ate, but also the crops they raised, processed, and cooked, as well as the grains and fruits they traded with others. There are many interesting examples of the work of archaeobotanists. For example, archaeobotanists conducting research in Jordan found that fig trees were domesticated nearly 11,400 years ago—making them the world's oldest known domesticated crop. Archaeobotanists working in the American Southwest have learned that the Hohokam culture grew a wide variety of domesticated crops such as corn, lima beans, squash, barley, and jackbeans, but also planted or utilized wild desert plants, such as cholla cactus and agave. In this setting and others, archaeobotanists use floatation processes to separate microscopic food fragments from the soil using running water or other fluids. Then they view them using a microscope. Testing and archaeological fieldwork may also indicate the type of foodstuffs the Hohokam stored for consumption during time periods when less food was available, and which they ate as soon as they were harvested. They have also found out that the Hohokam, a desert people, gathered acorns in more mountainous areas to supplement their desert diet.

The growing importance of phytolith analysis is also helping archaeobotanists conduct research. Phytoliths, which are microscopic pieces of silica, collect naturally in the cells of many types of plants. When a plant dies and begins to decay, phytoliths remain well preserved and turn hard as glass. Phytoliths are found in ash layers and hearths, but also inside pottery and plaster and on stone tools and animal teeth. Specialists have used phytolith microfossils to identify different varieties of wild maize dating back to pre-Columbian times. The oldest known phytoliths have been recovered from dinosaur dung dating back more than 70 million years.

Archaeopalynologists are specialized archaeobotanists who study pollen, dinoflagellates, spores, and related materials.

Underwater archaeobotany—mainly research conducted at shipwreck sites—is another subspecialty. Information gathered at such sites provides evidence of remains unlike those commonly found on land. One reason is that shipping jars or other containers used to transport goods, combined with cool temperatures, lack of sunlight, and layers of sediment, helped preserve the remains. Research done on a shipwreck found at Ulu Burun, Turkey, in the Mediterranean, revealed a great deal of information about people who lived during the Bronze Age. Archaeobotanists learned what types of food they ate and what foods they used in trade. Archaeobotanists found remains of fig seeds and olives and charred remains of different grains. They also discovered evidence of known luxury items at the time—fragments of pomegranate skins, impressions of different spices, and aromatic resins. Another interesting find was a group of copper ingots stacked on thorny burnet, a short, spiny bush. Thorny burnet had been found in other shipwrecks, but archaeologists were unsure of its use. The thorny burnet found on the Ulu Burun shipwreck suggest that this plant was used as a cushion between heavy loads (such as the ingots) and a ship's hull.

Geoarchaeologists study soil samples, rock formations, and other landforms to determine why people chose a certain area to live and their effects on the area. Geoarchaeologists may also investigate changing global climates or the availability of materials to make tools or cooking vessels or for building shelters and other structures. One recent geoarchaeological study even focused on shifts in North American coastlines in determining migration routes of people from neighboring continents before and during the Ice Age. Geoarchaeologists took into account the route's location alongside continental plate boundaries actively changing due to earthquakes, rising sea levels, shifting glaciers, and sedimentation and erosion—all possible scenarios of the time. Another interesting geoarchaeological study conducted in Tyson's Corners, Virginia, addressed the role of landscape during several Civil War battles. Specialists found that the topography of certain fields may have had an effect on the battle's outcome. Geoarchaeologists also study how battles changed the landscape.

In addition to conducting fieldwork, environmental archaeologists spend a considerable amount of time compiling research and writing papers and articles for professional archaeological journals. They meet with representatives of government agencies and private benefactors to obtain funding for their research. They may be asked to present their findings at symposiums or association conferences. Environmental archaeologists also work as teachers at colleges and universities and as curators at museums.

REQUIREMENTS

High School

In high school, pursue a college preparatory program. Take general classes in history, science, chemistry, and mathematics. You should also take courses in speech and English. Archaeologists must have excellent oral communication skills and be able to write detailed reports and scholarly articles about their findings. Foreign language skills will also help you in later research in other countries. Computer science courses will teach you how to use computers and work with many advanced technologies used during archaeological excavations.

If you are interested in becoming an environmental archaeologist, take classes in botany, earth science, biology, anatomy and physiology, geology, geography, and related subject areas.

Postsecondary Training

Most archaeology positions require applicants to have at least a master's degree, and a doctorate degree is necessary to obtain top positions in the field (including those at four-year colleges and universities). Archaeology departments are typically part of anthropology departments; few separate archaeology departments exist in U.S. colleges and universities.

Many aspiring environmental archaeologists earn undergraduate degrees in archaeology or anthropology. Others, who have chosen a specialty in the field may earn a degree in their chosen discipline—for example, zoology or biology if they plan to pursue a career in zooarchaeology, geology or geography if they are interested in geoarchaeology, and botany if they plan to pursue a career in archaeobotany.

Some colleges and universities offer graduate programs in environmental archaeology. The Archaeological Geology Division of the Geological Society of America offers a list of graduate programs in archaeological geology and geoarchaeology at its Web site, http://rock.geosociety.org/arch.

Underwater archaeobotanists must learn how to dive. Dive training is offered by colleges and universities, local dive shops, and PADI, a professional diving association.

Certification or Licensing

The Register of Professional Archaeologists offers voluntary registration to archaeologists who agree to "abide by an explicit code of conduct and standards of research performance; who hold a graduate degree in archaeology, anthropology, art history, classics, history, or another germane discipline; and who have substantial practical experience."

PADI offers voluntary certification to divers. Contact the organization for more information.

Other Requirements

Environmental archaeologists should be curious, detail oriented, patient, and enjoy solving problems. They should have excellent communication skills and be able to work as a member of an interdisciplinary team and on their own when necessary. Environmental archaeologists must be willing to work away from home for long periods when conducting field research. Underwater archaeobotanists need excellent diving skills and must have an understanding of the physical and biological elements—especially as they relate to the preservation of botanical artifacts.

EXPLORING

There are many ways to learn more about environmental archaeology and archaeology in general. You can read books and magazines, visit Web sites (such as Dr. Kitty Emery's Web site, http://www.environmental-archaeology.com), and take field trips to archaeology and natural history museums. You can also ask your school counselor to arrange an information interview with an environmental archaeologist.

You can learn more about geoarchaeology by joining the Archaeological Geology Division (Geological Society of America) & Geoarchaeology Interest Group on Facebook (http://www.facebook.com/group.php?gid=33028214313&_fb_noscript=1). You don't need to be an archaeologist to join the group. You just need to have an interest in learning more about geoarchaeology. Check out Facebook for other environmental archaeology-related groups.

EMPLOYERS

Environmental archaeologists are employed by universities and community colleges, contract archaeology companies, and laboratories. Others work for museums that may be independent or affiliated with universities. Federal government agencies, such as the National Park Service, also employ environmental archaeologists. Some archaeologists operate their own consulting firms.

STARTING OUT

Many archaeology graduate students gain experience in the field by participating in internships or working as research assistants or teaching fellows. This experience looks great on a resume and will help graduates land a job.

Career services offices and graduate school professors are excellent sources of job leads. Some professional associations provide job listings at their Web sites.

Some aspiring environmental archaeologists work in general archaeology positions while gaining experience via formal advanced education or via on-the-job experience.

ADVANCEMENT

Most archaeology teachers start as assistant professors, and move into associate professor and possibly full professor positions. Those working in museums also have an opportunity to advance within the institution in terms of higher pay or increased responsibility. Archaeologists working outside academia and museums will be promoted based on the advancement criteria of the individual companies and organizations for which they work.

EARNINGS

The U.S. Department of Labor (DOL) does not provide salary information for environmental archaeologists. Median annual earnings for all archaeologists were $53,460 in 2009, according to the DOL. Ten percent of archaeologists earned less than $31,530, and 10 percent earned $87,890 or more.

Many archaeologists work in academia. According to the DOL, college and university archaeology professors earned between $41,270 and $119,070 in 2009, depending on the type of institution. Median annual earnings were $69,520.

Full-time environmental archaeologists usually receive benefits such as vacation days, sick leave, health and life insurance, and a savings and pension program. Self-employed archaeologists must provide their own benefits.

WORK ENVIRONMENT

Work settings for environmental archaeologists vary by employer. Those who work in academia enjoy comfortable work settings. Those employed by laboratories work in clean, well-lit settings that are climate controlled. Archaeologists who conduct fieldwork may live in primitive conditions and work in all types of weather. They should be prepared to get dirty as they conduct research and explore archaeological sites. Underwater archaeobotanists work beneath the water in sometimes dangerous conditions.

OUTLOOK

Employment for archaeologists is expected to grow much faster than the average for all careers through 2018. Opportunities for environmental archaeologists should also be good. This specialty is in demand at archaeological digs today as archaeology professionals seek to gain a more comprehensive understanding of past cultures' interactions with the natural world. Opportunities should be best for environmental archaeologists with advanced training and many years of experience in the field.

FOR MORE INFORMATION

For information on palynology, contact
American Association of Stratigraphic Palynologists
http://www.palynology.org

For information on careers in biology, contact
American Institute of Biological Sciences
1444 I Street, NW, Suite 200
Washington, DC 20005-6535
Tel: 202-628-1500
http://www.aibs.org

For job listings and information on Environmental Archaeology:
The Journal of Human Palaeoecology, *contact*
Association for Environmental Archaeology
http://www.envarch.net

For information on careers, contact
Association of American Geographers
1710 16th Street, NW
Washington, DC 20009-3198
Tel: 202-234-1450

E-mail: gaia@aag.org
http://www.aag.org

To read Careers in Botany and Botany for the Next Millennium,
visit the society's Web site.
Botanical Society of America
PO Box 299
St. Louis, MO 63166-0299
Tel: 314-577-9566
E-mail: bsa-manager@botany.org
http://www.botany.org

For an overview of the career of archaeologist written by an associate professor of anthropology, visit
Frequently Asked Questions About a Career in Archaeology in the U.S.
http://www.museum.state.il.us/ismdepts/anthro/dlcfaq.html

For career information, contact
Geological Society of America
Archaeological Geology Division
PO Box 9140
Boulder, CO 80301-9140
Tel: 888-443-4472
E-mail: gsaservice@geosociety.org
http://www.geosociety.org
http://rock.geosociety.org/arch

For information on underwater archaeology, contact
Institute of Nautical Archaeology
PO Drawer HG
College Station, TX 77841-5137
Tel: 979-845-6694
E-mail: info@inadiscover.com
http://inadiscover.com

For more information on archaeozoology, contact
International Council for Archaeozoology
http://www.alexandriaarchive.org/icaz

For information on state archaeologists and archaeology museums
and resources, contact
National Association of State Archaeologists
http://www.uiowa.edu/~osa/nasa

For information on diving instruction and certification, contact
PADI
30151 Tomas Street
Rancho Santa Margarita, CA 92688-2125
Tel: 800-729-7234
http://www.padi.com/scuba

For information on professional registration, contact
Register of Professional Archaeologists
5024-R Campbell Boulevard
Baltimore, MD 21236-5943
Tel: 410-933-3486
E-mail: info@rpanet.org
http://www.rpanet.org

For information on archaeology careers and job listings, contact
Society for American Archaeology
900 Second Street, NE, Suite 12
Washington, DC 20002-3560
Tel: 202-789-8200
E-mail: headquarters@saa.org
http://www.saa.org

The SAS is an association for "those interested in advancing our knowledge of the past through a wide range of techniques deriving from the fields of physics, chemistry, and the natural sciences." Visit its Web site for more information.
Society for Archaeological Sciences (SAS)
http://www.socarchsci.org

For career information, contact
Society for Historical Archaeology
9707 Key West Avenue, Suite 100
Rockville, MD 20850-3992
Tel: 301-990-2454
E-mail: hq@sha.org
http://www.sha.org
http://www.sha.org/EHA/splash.cfm

For more information about ethnobiology, contact
Society of Ethnobiology
Department of Geography
University of North Texas

1155 Union Circle, #305279
Denton, TX 76203-5017
Tel: 940-565-4987
http://ethnobiology.org

INTERVIEW

Dr. Kitty Emery is an associate curator of environmental archaeology at the Florida Museum of Natural History, University of Florida in Gainesville, Florida. She is also a professor in the Department of Anthropology at the University of Florida. Dr. Emery discussed the field and her career with the editors of Careers in Focus: Archaeology.

Q. What is environmental archaeology?

A. Environmental archaeology is the interdisciplinary study of past human interactions with the natural world—a world that encompasses plants, animals, and landscapes. We seek to reconstruct ancient environments associated with archaeological sites and the use of plants, animals, and landscapes by the people who once inhabited these sites. We are interested in the impact people had on the world around them, and the way ancient peoples perceived and were affected by their surroundings the plants and animals on which they relied. Environmental archaeology is traditionally divided into three subfields: zooarchaeology (the study of animal remains), archaeobotany (the study of plant remains), and geoarchaeology (the study of the abiotic landscape). We use both modern comparative and archaeological collections in our research.

Q. Please describe a day in your life on the job. What are your typical work responsibilities? What is your work environment like?

A. My job as an environmental archaeology research curator in a museum and an anthropology professor in a university includes several "typical" workdays. On many days I teach classes to undergraduates and graduate students in an anthropology department, advise students on research projects, and mentor my graduate students in completing their specialized training. On other days, I spend my time surrounded by dusty piles of environmental artifacts from archaeological sites, comparing them to modern examples to identify and understand their meaning in the archaeological record. On still other "typical" days, I sweat under the tropical sun in Central America, excavating through the garbage of ancient peoples to discover the remains of their dinners and ritual events.

Q. What are the most important personal and professional qualities for environmental archaeologists?

A. An environmental archaeologist must be patient and detail oriented! Our initial research is time consuming and often seems a bit boring, examining endless bits of bone or pollen grains and laboriously counting and classifying. However, an environmental archaeologist must also be able to think broadly and innovatively, bringing together the boring data into a complex puzzle of big models, big questions, and unusual answers. We often work in a team made up of specialists from many fields and must be able to understand a wide array of techniques and methods to answer our questions. An environmental archaeologist must also be willing to get dirty—whether screening dusty back-dirt piles, dissecting smelly comparative animal specimens, or mucking through peat bogs in search of waterlogged plant specimens.

Q. What are some of the pros and cons of your job?

A. My job offers the satisfaction of revealing and learning about the way ancient peoples used and abused their natural environments, and passing that knowledge on to my students and the modern descendants of the people I study. It offers me the hope that we will be able to apply this knowledge to protect our own fragile environments and cultures. However, my job also includes the mundane difficulties of seeking funding to support this important research, maintaining good lab practice methods, and ensuring that my research is published. It also includes the complexities of seeking political support for environmental archaeology and reaching out to those very people who are sometimes the greatest abusers of environments and people. This can be very frustrating.

Q. What is the employment outlook for environmental archaeologists?

A. The jobs available to an environmental archaeologist are diverse and each requires a different level of training and specialization. With an undergraduate degree, environmental archaeology gives you a unique perspective on both environments and

cultures that is really useful for many service/outreach/envi-
ronmental jobs. An MA in environmental archaeology requires
a specialization in one of the subfields and therefore qualifies
you to do some fairly specific research. You would then be
eligible for jobs with contract archaeology companies, many
biological and environmental laboratories, and in such projects
as environmental or archaeological assessment. With a Ph.D.
in environmental archaeology, you open the door to work as
a professor or researcher. Those jobs are actually very rare
though they are the most rewarding in terms of flexibility for
pursuing the questions that most intrigue an environmental
archaeologist.

**Q. What have been some of your most rewarding experi-
ences in your career and why?**

A. My most rewarding experiences have been learning directly
from the people whose ancestors I study and introducing them
to their own ancestors in ways they had never imagined. We
always work with the local community when doing an excavation or pursuing a research question. They are direct rela-
tives, many hundreds of generations removed, of the culture
we are studying, and yet surprisingly often, don't even realize
it. As we work, we talk about the wonders of the past and the
importance of their own culture—and they teach me about the
fascinating modern practices and beliefs. Intriguingly, these are
often directly related. As we excavate terraces built more than
1,000 years ago, we chat about the difficulties they currently
have farming the land—imagine their interest in discovering
their ancestors used terraces to successfully farm for hundreds
of years, a technique now forgotten in the area. Imagine my
interest in hearing about the use of burned animal remains as
fertilizers today and recovering just such burned remains in
ancient terrace soils from the archaeological past.

Ethnoarchaeologists

QUICK FACTS

School Subjects
Foreign language
History

Personal Skills
Communication/ideas
Technical/scientific

Work Environment
Indoors and outdoors
Primarily multiple locations

Minimum Education Level
Master's degree

Salary Range
$31,530 to $53,460 to
$119,070+

Certification or Licensing
Voluntary

Outlook
About as fast as the average

DOT
054, 090

GOE
02.04.01, 12.03.02

NOC
4121, 4169

O*NET-SOC
19-3091.00, 19-3091.01,
19-3091.02, 25-1061.00

OVERVIEW

Ethnoarchaeologists study the material remains of contemporary cultures with the goal of understanding cultures of the past. They examine current customs and rituals, collect and study ancient and current artifacts, and talk to present-day cultural groups about their lifestyle. Based on their findings, ethnoarchaeologists hypothesize about a past culture's social organization, everyday life (hunting, cooking, religion, social customs, etc.), and history.

HISTORY

The term *ethnoarchaeology* was first used by the ethnographer and archaeologist Jesse Fewkes around 1900. He conducted ethoarchaeological studies at Mesa Verde and Tusayan Pueblo in the American Southwest, but he is probably best known for making recordings of the music and stories of the Passamaquoddy Indians of the American Northeast in 1890—the first recordings of their kind.

Since the beginning of the 20th century, ethnographers and anthropologists have studied "present day" civilizations to help interpret the past. But as time progressed many archaeologists came to believe that these professionals did not put enough emphasis on the materials remains of societies, which limited the amount of information that could be gathered. In the early 1970s, archaeologists began conducting this type of research. One significant example of this type of study is found in the work of pioneering ethnoarchaeologist Lewis Binford, according to *Archaeology Essentials: Theories, Methods, and Practice,* by Colin Renfrew and Paul Bahn. In the 1960s, Binford attempted to understand hunter-gatherer groups that lived in France 180,000–40,000 years ago. He realized that to help him understand past cultures, he should study current hunter-gatherer cultures. From 1969 to 1973, he lived among the Nunamiut Eskimo, a tribe of hunter-gatherers in Alaska. In the course of his fieldwork, Binford learned that hunter-gatherer cultures, regardless of the era in which they lived, shared many similar functions—such as how they set up their camps for optimum efficiency or how they butchered meat. For example, Binford found evidence to suggest that modern day Nunamiut Eskimo used the same, or at least very similar, butchering techniques as their prehistoric ancestors. He came to this conclusion after studying fragments of tools and bones found in ancient campsites in the Arctic. The bone fragments had distinctive mark patterns left from cutting tools that were similar to the patterns found in the modern day Eskimos' discarded bones left after a butchering session. Due to the extreme cold, Binford also found that modern day Eskimos butcher their game by the community campfire, as did their ancestors, as proven by discarded bones and garbage piles around the remains of an ancient fire pit. Other butchered parts were thrown a greater distance from the fire. Binford applied these and other findings to his study of ancient hunter-gatherer groups in France.

Other well-known ethnoarchaeologists include Susan Kent, who was known for her work in the American Southwest and southern Africa; Nicholas David, who has conducted fieldwork in Cameroon, Nigeria, Ghana, Sudan, and the Central African Republic; Carol Kramer, who conducted fieldwork in India and was a strong advocate for gender equity in anthropology; and Richard Gould, who has studied Aboriginal groups in Australia and is the inventor of *disaster archaeology,* in which archaeologists gather and scientifically study physical remains to determine what happened during a terrorist attack or an accident such as a fire.

Ethnoarchaeologists continue to comprise a small, but growing, subfield in archaeology. Their work helps shed light on both past and present cultures.

THE JOB

Ethnoarchaeologists generally perform the same or similar duties as traditional archaeologists, but focus more on studying the material culture of living human societies to understand how cultures of the past created, used, and discarded or reused objects or structures. Ethnoarchaeologists study many types of material cultural—from tools and building materials, to buildings and other structures, to ceramics, religious items, and even waste. To understand a past culture, they seek out a modern-day equivalent society that may have similar attributes. By interviewing members of the modern-day culture, observing them in their daily lives (hunting, preparing food, cooking, making pottery, tools, or weapons, etc.), and studying their material culture (discarded or broken pottery, tools, etc.), they can establish shared traits with ancient cultures.

The range of ethnoarchaeological studies is wide. The following paragraphs detail just a few recent studies conducted around the world.

Ethnoarchaeolgists in Cyprus studied village potters and learned that their production techniques closely matched those that were used in the area for more than 6,000 years. For example, they found that water jars and goat milking pots constructed in present-day Cyprus were similar to those found from the Cypriot Bronze Age. Few prehistoric pottery-making sites had been discovered in Cyprus, and the goal of the ethnoarchaeologists was to record present-day potters at work, create drawings of pottery-making areas, and collect samples from past and present production sites. The ethnoarchaeologists used this information to help them locate prehistoric production locations, which helped them understand the social and economic conditions of the ancient Cyprian culture.

Ethnoarchaeologists studied modern village households in Kalinga, Philippines, particularly in the methods of food preparation and ceramic vessel use. By analyzing food preparation and cooking techniques, the number of cooking vessels, and even midden deposits (community garbage pits), ethnoarchaeologists were able to gauge a relationship between kitchen tools and accessories and the size and composition of the household. In this study, the role of households within the community was also considered, especially the roles of extended families. Ethnoarchaeologists even considered the type of cooking pots, or their unique decoration. For example, it was found that several kitchens used large amounts of pottery manufactured in another village. While durability or function could have been a factor, this preference may also suggest a friendship or alliance between the two villages.

Ethnoarchaeologists also study the size and location of structures within a community or village. A study of Mayan pottery by ethnoarchaeologists is one example. By observing how modern Mexican villages created pottery and other ceramic goods, including the different facilities/structures used in various stages of production, ethnoarchaeologists were better able to understand the types or design of structures used to create, finish, or store the pottery goods of their Mayan forebearers. This information helped them as they searched for structures and artifacts at Mayan archaeological sites.

Words to Learn

Anthropomorphic: Artifacts and pieces of art that appear to feature humans.

Antiquities: Monuments and relics of ancient times (before the Middle Ages).

Artifact: An object made or changed by a human.

Cairn: Stones that have been arranged by humans.

Catalogue: Descriptions of artifacts recovered in archaeological research.

Culture: The way of life of a people (including customs, art, religion, behavioral patterns, etc.).

Ecofact: The remains of a natural item (such as a plant or animal) found at an archaeological site that provides information about the people who lived there.

Ethnography: A branch of anthropology dealing with the study of cultures.

Excavation: The systematic uncovering of archaeological materials by removing soil, leaves, stones, and other elements.

Excavation plan: A detailed plan for the careful excavation of an archaeological site.

Fieldwork: Research done on a specific site.

Hypothesis: An educated guess that can be tested.

Midden: A garbage pile; archaeologists study middens to learn about what past peoples ate and what items they used in daily life.

Native American Graves Protection and Repatriation Act: A federal law passed in 1990 that created a process for federal agencies and museums to return certain cultural items to Native American tribes or lineal descendants.

Provenience: The exact location of an artifact or feature at an archaeological site.

Realia: The remains of people, plants, and animals.

Remote sensing: A general term for survey techniques that don't disturb subsurface archaeological deposits.

Screening: Sifting dirt found at an archaeological site through a wire screen to locate artifacts or bone fragments.

Site: A place that shows signs of occupation by humans.

Because ethnoarchaeologists study other cultural groups, they often travel to conduct their research and talk to the local people. It is important that ethnoscientists are not intrusive when conducting research or fieldwork. They must always remember that they are acting as observers rather than agents of change.

In addition to field study, ethnoarchaeologists spend a great amount of time compiling research and writing papers and articles for professional archaeology journals. They may be asked to present their findings at symposiums or professional meetings. They also have to continuously seek out funding from private and government sources. Some ethnoarchaeologists may hold teaching positions or work as curators.

REQUIREMENTS

High School
Sociology courses will teach you the basics of research methods and observation techniques. If your school offers any anthropology classes, be sure to take them. Learning a foreign language can be helpful if you conduct field research. The foreign language you take in high school may not be the one you will need later, but learning a second language should make it easier for you to learn others. History and art classes will expose you to the cultures of different peoples of the world. Any classes that highlight the value of cultural diversity will be useful. Mathematics and computer science classes are also helpful.

Postsecondary Training
You will need at least a master's degree in anthropology or archaeology to work in nonacademic settings. To teach at the university level, you will need a Ph.D. in cultural anthropology or a related field. Some schools offer concentrations or courses in ethnoarchaeology. For example, Grinnell College in Iowa offers a course called Experimental Archaeology and Ethnoarchaeology, which "examines the theoretical basis and practice of experimental archaeology and ethnoarchaeology" and includes lab work and research projects. Classes in archaeology, linguistics, history, sociology, religion, and mythology can help prepare you to work with indigenous peoples.

Certification or Licensing
The Register of Professional Archaeologists offers voluntary registration to archaeologists who agree to "abide by an explicit code of conduct and standards of research performance; who hold a graduate degree in archaeology, anthropology, art history, classics, history, or another germane discipline; and who have substantial practical experience."

Other Requirements
Ethnoarchaeologists should be open to learning about other cultures and be able to accept lifestyles and customs that are different from

their own. A nonjudgmental nature is key for success in this field. Many cultural groups of the world live lives that are far less technologically oriented than in the Western world. Ethnoarchaeologists embrace those differences.

Ethnoarchaeologists need a healthy curiosity and should enjoy research. They should be able to work independently and as part of a team. Good communication and interpersonal skills are key to success in this career.

Many ethnoarchaeologists are away from home for extended periods and must be able to tolerate different climates, rustic accommodations, unusual foods, and other physical conditions. Adaptability is a key personality trait for ethnoarchaeologists doing fieldwork.

EXPLORING

Explore extracurricular, volunteer, or part-time opportunities that will give you some background experience in archaeology. You can visit Web sites that discuss archaeology and ethnoarchaeology; participate in summer programs offered by colleges and historical organizations; and read books and magazines about the field. Museums offer a wealth of information on different cultures, including exhibits, reading materials, lectures, and workshops.

Take any opportunity offered you to travel, particularly to nonindustrialized countries and more remote areas of the world that have been less influenced by Western culture. Explore study-abroad programs or consider volunteering with the Peace Corps to get an intense, long-term experience living in another culture.

Visit the Web sites of professional organizations, such as the American Society for Ethnohistory, the American Anthropological Association, the Society for American Archaeology, the Society for Applied Anthropology, and the Society for Historical Archaeology. (See For More Information for the Web links.)

EMPLOYERS

Ethnoarchaeologists work in the same places as other social and life scientists—universities, research institutes, government and nongovernment organizations, museums, and historical societies. Sometimes ethnoscientists become independent consultants.

STARTING OUT

While working on your degree, be sure to communicate your interests to your professors. They may be aware of opportunities at the university or elsewhere. You might be able to participate in a university research project or become a research assistant or teaching fellow. Professional organizations are another important resource when it comes to finding a job. If you network with others in your field, you have a good chance of hearing about job opportunities. Also, organizations might post information on jobs, internships, or fellowships in their journals or on their Web sites.

There is strong competition for academic positions. Most students begin their job search while finishing their graduate degrees. Your first position is likely to be an instructor in general courses in anthropology, history, or archaeology. In order to advance to higher ranks of professor, you will be required to do research, during which you can focus on your ethnoscience specialty. Because research opportunities are difficult to come by, you might have to create your own opportunities, perhaps by proposing research projects.

ADVANCEMENT

Ethnoarchaeologists advance by producing high quality research and publishing articles or books. They might come to be known as experts in their field. They might become the head of a research project. The advancement path of ethnoarchaeologists who teach in universities is instructor to assistant professor to associate professor to full professor. A full professor might eventually become a department head.

A related career is that of *ethnohistorian*, who researches the history of various cultures, such as Native Americans and other non-European peoples. They study maps, music, paintings, photography, folklore, oral tradition, ecology, archaeological sites and materials, museum collections, enduring customs, language, and place names.

EARNINGS

The U.S. Department of Labor reports that the median annual salary for anthropologists and archaeologists was $53,460 in 2009. Salaries ranged from less than $31,530 to $87,890 or more. Salaries for college and university anthropology professors ranged from less than $41,270 for the lowest paid 10 percent to more than $119,070 for the highest paid 10 percent during that same year. The median salary for these professors was $69,520.

Ethnoarchaeologists who work full time for colleges and universities and other employers usually receive benefits such as vacation days, sick leave, health and life insurance, and a savings and pension program. Self-employed ethnoarchaeologists must provide their own benefits.

WORK ENVIRONMENT

Ethnoarchaeologists in academia mainly work indoors, but also may conduct research in the field. Their time is spent teaching, meeting with students, writing texts or grant proposals, or compiling and analyzing data. Some of the most challenging aspects of working as an academic are obtaining tenure and obtaining financial support so that they can conduct fieldwork. Ethnoarchaeologists often conduct fieldwork outdoors. When in the field, ethnoarchaeologists encounter climates that are different from their own, such as the tropical rainforest or the Arctic tundra. Ethnoarchaeologists must be willing to work outdoors, sometimes for long periods of time, no matter what the weather, and they must be prepared to stay in primitive living conditions.

OUTLOOK

The *Occupational Outlook Handbook* reports that employment for anthropologists and archaeologists will grow much faster than the average for all careers through 2018. Employment for ethnoarchaeologists is not expected to be as strong. This is a very small field and many ethnoarchaeologists work in this specialty while working in other archaeological specialties and/or as college professors.

Overall employment for postsecondary teachers in general will grow faster than the average for all occupations through 2018. This is largely because enrollment is expected to increase, creating a greater need for professors.

While interest may increase in ethnoarchaeology, it is difficult to say whether funding will increase as well. If there are federal budget cuts or if colleges are forced to reduce funding for research, there might be a decrease in the amount of money devoted to new research projects, or existing projects might not get renewed.

FOR MORE INFORMATION

The following organization offers valuable information about anthropological careers and student associations:
American Anthropological Association
2200 Wilson Boulevard, Suite 600
Arlington, VA 22201-3357
Tel: 703-528-1902
http://www.aaanet.org

For information on careers and a list of graduate programs in anthropology, contact
American Association of Physical Anthropologists
http://www.physanth.org

For background information on the field of ethnohistory along with links to schools offering ethnohistory courses, visit
American Society for Ethnohistory
http://ethnohistory.org

For information on archaeological careers and job listings, contact
Society for American Archaeology
900 Second Street, NE, Suite 12
Washington, DC 20002-3560
Tel: 202-789-8200
E-mail: headquarters@saa.org
http://www.saa.org

The SfAA Web site has career listings and publications for those wanting to read more about current topics in the social sciences.
Society for Applied Anthropology (SfAA)
PO Box 2436
Oklahoma City, OK 73101-2436
Tel: 405-843-5113
E-mail: info@sfaa.net
http://www.sfaa.net

For career information, contact
Society for Historical Archaeology
9707 Key West Avenue, Suite 100
Rockville, MD 20850-3992
Tel: 301-990-2454
E-mail: hq@sha.org
http://www.sha.org

For more information about ethnobiology, contact
Society of Ethnobiology
Department of Geography
University of North Texas
1155 Union Circle, #305279
Denton, TX 76203-5017
Tel: 940-565-4987
http://ethnobiology.org

Field Technicians and Supervisors

OVERVIEW

Field technicians perform a variety of duties at archaeological digs. They are often students in baccalaureate degree programs or those who have earned a bachelor's degree in archaeology, anthropology, or a related field. *Field supervisors* manage archaeology fieldwork projects and those who staff them. They typically have at least a master's degree in archaeology, anthropology, or a related discipline. For some positions, substantial experience in the field may be substituted for formal educational training. Field technicians and supervisors work at archaeological digs that are located in rural and urban areas. Sites are located in fields, in the mountains, in deserts, in caves, under city streets, and in many other settings. Archaeological sites also are located beneath water, such as the sites of shipwrecks or submerged cities.

HISTORY

Formal archaeological research in the United States did not begin until the late 18th century. Early archaeologists typically handled most of the site surveying, site clearing, excavation, artifact analysis, and cataloging themselves. As more archaeological sites were discovered and work at them became more demanding, field technicians with some training in archaeology, anthropology, or a related field were needed to work as "diggers" on projects. And as more workers were added at sites, it became necessary to hire managers to oversee

QUICK FACTS

School Subjects
Earth science
Geography
History

Personal Skills
Following instructions
Technical/scientific

Work Environment
Indoors and outdoors
Primarily multiple locations

Minimum Education Level
Bachelor's degree

Salary Range
$20,800 to $46,800 to
$93,600+

Certification or Licensing
Voluntary

Outlook
Faster than the average

DOT
N/A

GOE
N/A

NOC
N/A

O*NET-SOC
N/A

A technician with the Kentucky Archaeological Survey uses ground-penetrating radar to look for unmarked graves around a battle monument in the Frankfort Cemetery in Frankfort, Kentucky. *(Patti Longmire, AP Photo)*

their work. This allowed more experienced archaeologists to focus on the actual scientific studies associated with the dig.

Today, field technicians and supervisors are important members of archaeology crews. These positions provide an excellent way for people to break into the field and gain experience.

THE JOB

Field technicians at archaeological field sites have many different responsibilities. These duties vary based on their level of experience, employer, and the type of archaeology project. Some typical job duties include conducting archaeological surveys, collecting samples, screening soil and sand for the presence of artifacts and remains, clearing vegetation from archaeological sites, laying out grid points and reference points, using global positioning system (GPS) and geographic information system (GIS) units and other types of technology to gather information about and map archaeological sites, using hand tools and other tools to excavate sites, taking photographs and videos of sites and artifacts, making sketches and drawings of sites and artifacts, recording archaeological features (such as fire pits, artifacts, bones, graves, walls, or garbage pits), washing and otherwise cleaning artifacts, testing artifacts and remains, conserving finds, cataloging and preparing archaeological artifact inventories, documenting field work on state historic preservation office forms and completing other paperwork, and creating databases of artifacts and remains.

Many field technicians and supervisors work for cultural resources management and contract archaeology firms. Cultural resources archaeology involves the identification of archaeological sites for protection under local, state, or federal laws before a construction project begins. At the federal level, sites are assessed to determine if they should be protected and placed on the National Register of Historic Places (http://www.nps.gov/nr).

There are three main phases of cultural resources archaeology. In Phase I, technicians, supervisors, and other archaeology professionals review the plans for a proposed construction site to see if any known archaeological sites are located on site. Then they go to the construction site and perform a walk-through to locate possible archaeological sites. They may also perform shovel tests in various areas. A shovel test is a very small excavation that determines if artifacts and/or remains are present. If significant archaeological evidence is discovered, the construction project may be altered before it progresses any further to protect these resources. In Phase II, more substantial excavations are performed in areas where artifacts were discovered on the surface. These tests are done to determine if significant collections of artifacts (called cultural deposits) are present. In Phase III, field technicians and supervisors conduct large-scale excavations to collect artifacts and related objects, as well as study the site, before construction begins; this is known as contract archaeology. In these instances, field technicians and supervisors need to work quickly because construction schedules may dictate that work start as soon as possible. After Phase III is completed, technicians analyze and conserve the recovered items and write detailed reports about their findings. By law, these reports must be submitted to government agencies.

In addition to working in the field, some technicians work in archaeology laboratories. This is also true for supervisors, who may be asked to work as laboratory managers concurrently with their fieldwork duties or during the winter when archaeological fieldwork slows down or completely stops (depending on the geographic location).

Typical tools and equipment used by field technicians and supervisors include shovels, trowels, dental picks, picks, mattocks, fine brushes, screens, flotation machines, coring tools, soil probes, bucket augers, metal detectors, flagging tape, pins and stakes, string/rope, rulers, measuring tape, line levels, compasses, clipboards, pen and paper, digital cameras, video recorders, GPS and GIS units, plastic bags, magnifying glasses, wheelbarrows, basic tools like screwdrivers and pliers, and plastic sheeting to protect sites and equipment from bad weather. Field technicians and supervisors also may use heavy earth-moving equipment such as backhoes, front-end loaders, scraper pans, and hydraulic excavators.

REQUIREMENTS

High School

To prepare for a career as a field technician or supervisor, you should pursue a college preparatory curriculum that includes courses in mathematics, statistics, and science. Computer science courses will be useful since many technicians and supervisors create maps using computer software. Additionally, courses in English and speech will help you develop the communication skills necessary for writing reports and getting along with coworkers. Take as many classes in archaeology, anthropology, and history that are offered.

Postsecondary Training

A minimum of a bachelor's degree in archaeology, anthropology, cultural resources, historic preservation, or a related major is required to work as a field technician. Some technicians also complement their degree by earning an archaeology technician certificate, which is offered by some two- and four-year colleges. Typical courses include Physical Anthropology, Introduction to Cultural Anthropology, Introduction to Archaeology, World Ethnography, Archaeological Methods, Archaeological Field Methods, and Internship or Field Work in Archaeology.

Field supervisors usually need a master's degree in archaeology, anthropology, cultural resources, historic preservation, or a related major, although some companies may hire applicants with only a bachelor's degree, but considerable experience. Most archaeology departments are typically part of anthropology departments. More than 350 colleges and universities have anthropology departments. While in college, be sure to participate in an internship or archaeological fieldwork. Many employers require that applicants have attended field school. A list of opportunities can be found at the Archaeological Institute of America's Web site, http://www.archaeo logical.org/webinfo.php?page=10016.

Certification or Licensing

Field technicians who use photogrammetry and remote sensing technologies can obtain voluntary certification from the American Society for Photogrammetry and Remote Sensing. Contact the society for more information.

The Register of Professional Archaeologists offers voluntary registration to archaeologists who agree to "abide by an explicit code of conduct and standards of research performance; who hold a graduate degree in archaeology, anthropology, art history, classics, history, or another germane discipline; and who have substantial practical experience."

Other Requirements

To be a successful field technician, you must be able to follow instructions and be patient, orderly, systematic, accurate, and objective in your work. You must be willing to work as a member of a team and operate independently, when necessary. Because of the increasing technical nature of archaeological fieldwork, you must have computer skills to be able to use highly complex equipment such as GPS and GIS technologies. Some employers require applicants to demonstrate proficiency with computer software programs such as Microsoft Word and Excel. Others require basic skill in photography or videography.

Field supervisors must have strong leadership and communications skills. They must be highly organized and able to give clear instructions and manage staff and resources. They must be able to juggle a variety of tasks at one time and make good decisions under pressure.

Field technicians and supervisors should be in good physical condition. Excavation work can be demanding, and workers may have to hike in and out of sites through rough terrain.

Some companies require field technicians and supervisors to have a valid driver's license and pass drug and background checks.

EXPLORING

To explore your interest in archaeology, read books about the field. Here are a few suggestions: *Archaeology For Dummies,* by Nancy Marie White (Hoboken, N.J.: For Dummies, 2008); *Archaeology Essentials: Theories, Methods and Practice,* by Paul Bahn and Colin Renfrew (London, U.K.: Thames & Hudson, 2007); and *Archaeology,* 5th ed., by Robert L. Kelly and David Hurst Thomas (Florence, Ky.: Wadsworth Publishing, 2009). Read archaeology-related publications that are geared for the general public, such as *American Archaeology* (http://www.americanarchaeology.com/aamagazine. html) and *Archaeology* (http://www.archaeology.org).

Check out Web sites, too. One suggestion: the National Park Service's Archaeology Program Web site, http://www.nps.gov/archeology.

The U.S. Forest Service offers Passport in Time, a "volunteer archaeology and historic preservation program...where volunteers work with professional Forest Service archaeologists and historians on national forests throughout the U.S. on such diverse activities as archaeological survey and excavation, rock art restoration, survey, archival research, historic structure restoration, oral history gathering, and analysis and curation of artifacts." Visit http://www.pass portintime.com for more information.

EMPLOYERS

Field technicians and supervisors are employed by cultural resources management firms, salvage archaeology companies, museums, colleges and universities, government agencies (such as the National Park Service and state historic preservation offices), and any other employer that conducts archaeological fieldwork.

STARTING OUT

Contact your school's career services office for help in arranging job interviews. Employers of archaeology field technicians often send recruiters to schools before graduation and arrange to employ promising graduates. Some community or technical colleges have work-study programs that provide cooperative part-time or summer work for pay. Employers involved with these programs often hire students full time after graduation.

The career of field supervisor is not an entry-level position. Most companies require that supervisors have three to five years of experience in archaeological fieldwork (with supervisory experience a plus).

Technicians and supervisors who want to work in the private sector should contact cultural resources management firms and other employers directly.

To learn more about opportunities with the federal government, contact your local Federal Job Information Center or the federal Office of Personnel Management (http://www.usajobs.gov) for application information. Details on opportunities with state and local agencies can be obtained by contacting these organizations directly.

Professional associations and organizations that offer job listings at their Web sites include the Archaeological Institute of America (http://www.archaeological.org), the Society for Historical Archaeology (http://www.sha.org/students_jobs), and the Society for American Archaeology (http://www.saa.org).

ADVANCEMENT

Possibilities for advancement are linked to levels of formal education and experience. As technicians gain experience and technical knowledge, they can advance to positions of greater responsibility and eventually work as supervisors. To become supervisors, technicians will most likely need a master's degree and several years of experience.

Field supervisors advance by taking on more managerial duties or by working for larger companies that pay higher salaries.

Many technicians and supervisors go on to earn master's and doctorates in archaeology, which qualify them to teach at colleges and universities.

EARNINGS

According to a 2009 salary survey by the American Cultural Resources Association, field technicians with at least a bachelor's degree and some experience earned hourly wages that ranged from $10 to $22.50 an hour (or $20,800 to $46,800 annually based on a 40-hour-a-week schedule) in 2009. Field supervisors earned hourly salaries that ranged from $13 to $45 (or $27,040 to $93,600 or more annually).

Technicians also receive a per diem rate that covers meals, transportation (at some companies), and other expenses. Per diem rates range from $30 to $40. Most companies provide free housing (which can range from a simple motel room to a primitive tent camp near an archaeological dig).

Benefits include paid vacation, health, disability, life insurance, and retirement or pension plans. Field technicians and supervisors who work on short-term, freelance projects do not receive benefits and must provide their own health insurance.

WORK ENVIRONMENT

Archaeology field technicians and supervisors usually work about 40 hours a week except when overtime is necessary. Some companies may have alternate work schedules. For example, a company may require technicians and supervisors to work 10 consecutive 10-hour days and then provide four or five days off until the cycle begins again. The peak work period for many kinds of archaeological work is during the summer months when weather conditions are most favorable. However, archaeological work crews are exposed to all types of weather conditions. Additionally, some field technicians may work as laboratory testing technicians during the winter months or other times where less fieldwork is conducted.

Archaeological fieldwork sites range from rugged, nearly inaccessible terrain in deserts or mountains to city centers that are surrounded by traffic, pedestrians, and other aspects of urban life.

Some archaeological field projects involve certain hazards depending upon the region and the climate as well as local plant and animal life. Field crews may encounter poisonous snakes and lizards, dangerous animals such as grizzly bears and wolves, and poisonous plants. They are subject to heat exhaustion, sunburn, and frostbite (although most archaeological digs shut down once it begins to snow and the ground freezes).

Work locations for field technicians and supervisors change frequently. Many technicians and supervisors are away from home for long periods of time. Some enjoy the vagabond lifestyle of a field worker so much that they do not even have a permanent address.

OUTLOOK

Employment for archaeologists is expected to grow much faster than the average for all careers through 2018, according to the U.S. Department of Labor. There will be many opportunities for field technicians and supervisors—especially in the fields of cultural resources management archaeology and salvage archaeology.

The need to replace workers who have retired, transferred to other occupations, or advanced to higher level archaeology careers will provide many opportunities. In general, technicians and supervisors with more education, skill training, and experience will have more job options.

FOR MORE INFORMATION

For information on certification and photogrammetry and remote sensing techniques used in the field of archaeology, contact
American Society for Photogrammetry and Remote Sensing
5410 Grosvenor Lane, Suite 210
Bethesda, MD 20814-2160
Tel: 301-493-0290
E-mail: asprs@asprs.org
http://www.asprs.org

For information on careers and publications, contact
Archaeological Institute of America
656 Beacon Street, 6th Floor
Boston, MA 02215-2006
Tel: 617-353-9361
E-mail: aia@aia.bu.edu
http://www.archaeological.org

*To learn about educational programs, fellowships, and employment
and volunteer opportunities, contact*
Archaeological Research Institute
Arizona State University
Tempe, AZ 85287-2402
Tel: 480-965-9231
http://www.archaeology.asu.edu

*For job postings, to participate in online career-related discussions,
and to access a list of archaeological fieldwork resources, visit the
following Web site:*
Archaeology Fieldwork
http://www.archaeologyfieldwork.com/AFW

*For an overview of the career of archaeologist written by an associ-
ate professor of anthropology, visit*
**Frequently Asked Questions About a Career in Archaeology in
the U.S.**
http://www.museum.state.il.us/ismdepts/anthro/dlcfaq.html

*For information on professional registration for archaeologists,
contact*
Register of Professional Archaeologists
5024-R Campbell Boulevard
Baltimore, MD 21236-5943
Tel: 410-933-3486
E-mail: info@rpanet.org
http://www.rpanet.org

For information on archaeological careers and job listings, contact
Society for American Archaeology
900 Second Street, NE, Suite 12
Washington, DC 20002-3560
Tel: 202-789-8200
E-mail: headquarters@saa.org
http://www.saa.org

The SAS is an association for "those interested in advancing our knowledge of the past through a wide range of techniques deriving from the fields of physics, chemistry, and the natural sciences." Visit its Web site for more information.

Society for Archaeological Sciences (SAS)
http://www.socarchsci.org

For career information, contact
Society for Historical Archaeology
9707 Key West Avenue, Suite 100
Rockville, MD 20850-3992
Tel: 301-990-2454
E-mail: hq@sha.org
http://www.sha.org
http://www.sha.org/EHA/splash.cfm

Forensic Anthropologists and Archaeologists

OVERVIEW

The American Academy of Forensic Sciences defines forensic science as any science that is "used in public, in a court, or in the justice system." *Forensic anthropologists* examine and identify bones and skeletal remains for the purposes of homicide, scientific, archaeological, or judicial investigations. *Forensic archaeologists* are specialized anthropologists who find and excavate human remains, evidence (weapons, cell phones, etc.), and other objects at crime scenes and accident sites. Only a very small percentage of anthropologists and archaeologists specialize in forensic science.

HISTORY

Forensic anthropology is a relatively new scientific discipline. Thomas Dwight is considered to be the father of forensic anthropology. He was an anatomist and educator at Harvard College, Bowdoin College, and Harvard Medical School. At Harvard's Warren Museum of Anatomy, Dwight created a section on osteology, the study of human bones. He developed an international reputation as an anatomist and wrote several books on the field including *Frozen Sections of a Child* (1872) and *Clinical Atlas of Variations of the Bones of the Hands and Feet* (1907). But despite Dwight's early work in the field, it wasn't until the 1930s that

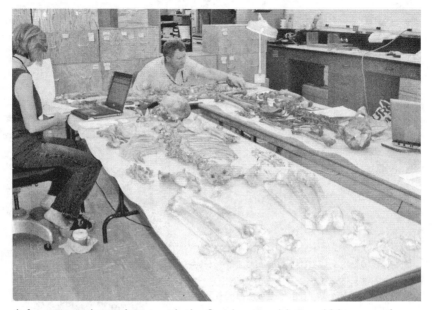

A forensic anthropologist with the Smithsonian National Museum of Natural History in Washington, D.C. (*right*) and his assistant examine skeletal remains exhumed from the Fort Craig cemetery in New Mexico. *(AP Photo/Courtesy of Lisa Croft, U.S. Bureau of Reclamation)*

police and organizations began turning to physical anthropologists to help solve grisly murders, which were often perpetuated by organized crime gangs.

The field underwent major advances during World War II and the Korean War. Hundreds of thousands of soldiers were killed during action, and forensic anthropologists were needed to identify the dead using health information gathered from the soldiers before they shipped off to battle.

Until the 1980s, most bodies and evidence at crime and accident scenes were quickly removed for study in a laboratory. This approach sometimes caused the loss of or mixing of evidence. To address these issues, law enforcement professionals began to seek out the services of archaeologists trained in forensic science to carefully excavate and document remains and other objects at crime and accident scenes.

Today, forensic anthropologists and archaeologists are in strong demand by law enforcement agencies, human rights groups, government agencies, and other organizations.

THE JOB

Forensic archaeologists play an important role in accident and criminal investigations, as well as in civil cases in which buried evidence (former fence lines, etc.) is involved.

When a crime is committed or suspected, forensic archaeologists help law enforcement officials locate crime scenes (typically gravesites) by using sensing devices or by performing visual surveys that identify possible sites. These crime scenes may contain human and animal remains, tools, weapons, cell phones, or other objects that belonged to the victim or perpetrators. Once they locate a grave, forensic archaeologists organize the area using a grid system and carefully record what they find in each grid. Then they use standard archaeological methods to excavate the grave. They record every possible detail about the grave and body before the remains are removed. This includes the type of soil in the grave; any evidence, weapons, or tools that were left in the area; the soil level of the grave and at what level each piece of evidence and the body was located; and anything other information that may help authorities solve the case. When these steps are complete, the archaeologist removes the remains and any other evidence from the grave and prepares it for transport to a crime laboratory for study by forensic anthropologists and other professionals.

Forensic archaeologists are also called on to provide expertise and assistance in response to war crimes where mass graves might have been created and in the aftermath of plane crashes, fires, or terrorist attacks such as the World Trade Center bombing.

Forensic anthropologists examine the bones and skeletal remains recovered by archaeologists to help identify the individual. (Other types of evidence, such as weapons, are analyzed by *evidence technicians* and *forensic scientists*.) They carefully clean the bones to make analysis easier and patiently examine and study them for any possible identifying information.

After first making sure that the bones being examined are those of a human, forensic anthropologists make observations and measurements, using tools such as magnifying glasses, microscopes, and calipers, that can give them a great deal of information about whose bones they are studying. This information can include the person's gender (there is a weight and size difference between male and female bones), age (less-complete bone development indicates a younger person, evidence of arthritis suggests that the individual is older, etc.), race (via known differences in nose and eye socket structure among different races), height and body type (which can be calculated based on the size of specific bones), and other unique features. Data from this type of analysis, when checked against information on missing-persons lists, played an important role in helping police identify many of the victims of serial killer John Wayne Gacy in the late 1970s.

Those with additional knowledge of *forensic entomology* (the scientific study of insect evidence) can also help pinpoint the time of death. Some forensic anthropologists specialize in facial reproduction, which is the art of attempting to re-create the appearance of a person's face.

Many forensic anthropologists and archaeologists are employed by academic or research institutions and are called in to work on cases when tragedies such as plane crashes, terrorist attacks, or natural disasters occur. Others work for law enforcement agencies, medical examiner's offices, or for the military. Forensic anthropologists and archaeologists are also often called upon to testify in court about their findings.

REQUIREMENTS

High School

Follow your high school's college prep program to be prepared for undergraduate and graduate programs in anthropology and/or archaeology. You should study English composition and literature to develop your writing and interpretation skills. Foreign language skills will also help you in later research and language study. Take classes in computers and classes in sketching, simple surveying, and photography to prepare for some of the demands of fieldwork. Mathematics and science courses can help you develop the skills you'll need in analyzing information and statistics.

Participation in science clubs and competitions will give you a general introduction to the scientific terms, investigative techniques, and laboratory practices that are used by scientists.

Postsecondary Training

You should be prepared for a long training period beyond high school. Most forensic anthropologists and archaeologists have at least a master's degree, but more often a doctorate in anthropology or archaeology. This course of study entails about four to 10 years of work beyond the bachelor's degree. You'll also need a doctorate in order to join the faculty of college and university anthropology and archaeology programs. Before beginning graduate work, you will study such basic courses as psychology, sociology, history, geography, mathematics, logic, English composition, and literature, as well as modern and ancient languages. The final two years of the undergraduate program will provide an opportunity for specialization not only in anthropology or archaeology but also in some specific phase of the discipline (in this instance, forensic science).

In starting graduate training, you should select an institution that has a good program in the area in which you hope to specialize. This is important, not only because the training should be of a high quality, but also because most graduates in anthropology or archaeology will receive their first jobs through their graduate universities. The American Association of Physical Anthropologists offers a list of graduate programs in physical anthropology at its Web site, http://www.physanth.org/career/departmental-graduate-programs-in-physical-anthropology.

Assistantships and temporary positions may be available to holders of bachelor's or master's degrees, but are usually available only to those working toward a doctorate.

Because this type of work may be sporadic, students interested in the profession should seek to ensure that they have other career options by obtaining an undergraduate education that covers a wide range of topics in physical anthropology or general archaeology.

Certification or Licensing
The American Board of Forensic Anthropology awards certification to forensic anthropologists who have a Ph.D., demonstrate experience in the field, and pass a practical and written examination. Contact the board for more information.

The Register of Professional Archaeologists offers voluntary registration to archaeologists who agree to "abide by an explicit code of conduct and standards of research performance; who hold a graduate degree in archaeology, anthropology, art history, classics, history, or another germane discipline; and who have substantial practical experience."

Other Requirements
To be a successful forensic scientists, you should enjoy solving problems. You should be able to work as a member of a team, as well as conduct research entirely on your own. Forensic anthropologists and archaeologists often work with forensic pathologists, odontologists, and homicide investigators on a case. Because much of your career will involve study and research, you should have great curiosity and a desire for knowledge. Forensic anthropologists and archaeologists

who testify in court need excellent communication skills. All workers need good writing skills in order to document their findings.

EXPLORING

General anthropology (which includes the subspecialty of archaeology) may be explored in a number of ways. Local amateur anthropological or archaeology societies may have weekly or monthly meetings and guest speakers, study developments in the field, and engage in exploration on the local level.

Trips to museums also will introduce you to the world of anthropology. Both high school and college students may work in museums on a part-time basis during the school year or during summer vacations.

If you are interested in forensic anthropology or forensic archaeology, you should read books and periodicals about the field. Ask your science teacher to arrange an information interview with a forensic anthropologist or archaeologist. You can learn more about forensic anthropology by visiting ForensicAnthro.com (http://www.forensicanthro.com) and forensic archaeology by visiting ForensicArchaeology.org (http://forensicarchaeology.org).

EMPLOYERS

Forensic anthropologists are employed by research institutions, colleges and universities, medical examiner's offices, law enforcement agencies, human rights organizations, and the military. Typical employers for forensic archaeologists include local and state law enforcement agencies, colleges and universities, the Federal Bureau of Investigation and other federal agencies, private human rights organizations, and the Joint MIA/POW Accounting Command of the U.S. Army. Most forensic anthropologists and archaeologists are employed as independent consultants.

STARTING OUT

The most promising way to gain entry into this occupation is through graduate school. Graduates might be approached prior to graduation by prospective employers. Often, professors will provide you with introductions as well as recommendations. You may have an opportunity to work as a research assistant or a teaching fellow while in graduate school, and frequently this experience is of tremendous help in qualifying for a job in another institution.

You should also be involved in internships to gain experience. These internship opportunities may be available through your graduate program, or you may have to seek them out yourself. Many organizations can benefit from the help of an anthropology or archaeology student; health centers, government agencies, and human rights groups all conduct research.

Additionally, many professional associations offer job listings at their Web sites. Visit the Web sites of the American Anthropological Association (http://www.aaanet.org/profdev), the American Association of Physical Anthropologists (http://www.physanth.org/job-postings), and Society for American Archaeology (http://www.saa.org/Careers/JobAnnouncements/tabid/256/Default.aspx) for job listings.

ADVANCEMENT

Advancement may be somewhat limited because the field of anthropology is very small. Most people beginning their teaching careers in colleges or universities will start as instructors and eventually advance to assistant professor, associate professor, and possibly full professor. Researchers on the college level have an opportunity to head research areas and to gain recognition among colleagues as an expert in many areas of study. Anthropologists and archaeologists employed in museums also have an opportunity to advance within the institution in terms of raises in salary or increases in responsibility and job prominence. Those anthropologists and archaeologists working outside academia and museums will be promoted according to the standards of the individual companies and organizations for which they work.

The fields of forensic anthropology and forensic archaeology are very small, and many people work part time. Advancement for forensic anthropologists and archaeologists who are salaried employees typically involves increases in salary and job duties. Self-employed forensic anthropologists and archaeologists can advance by becoming recognized experts in the field, and be asked to work on high-profile cases.

EARNINGS

The U.S. Department of Labor does not provide salary information for forensic anthropologists and archaeologists, but it does report that the median annual salary for all anthropologists and archeologists was $53,460 in 2009. Salaries ranged from less than $31,530 to $87,890 or more. Forensic anthropologists and archaeologists who work as consultants typically earn $100 to $200 an hour.

According to the U.S. Department of Labor, college and university anthropology and archaeology professors earned between $41,270 and $119,070 in 2009, depending on the type of institution. The median salary for these professors was $9,520.

Benefits for full-time workers include vacation and sick time, health, and sometimes dental, insurance, and pension or 401(k) plans. Self-employed forensic anthropologists and archaeologists must provide their own benefits.

WORK ENVIRONMENT

The majority of forensic anthropologists and archaeologists are employed by colleges and universities, medical examiner's offices, and law enforcement agencies and, as such, have good working conditions, although fieldwork may require extensive travel and difficult living conditions (especially for archaeologists). Educational facilities are normally clean, well lighted, and ventilated.

Full-time forensic anthropologists and archaeologists work about 40 hours a week, and the hours may be irregular. Forensic anthropologists and archaeologists must be able to handle unpleasant sights and smells such as decomposing flesh, trauma to the human body, bodily fluids, and maggots and other insects. Physical strength and stamina is necessary for fieldwork. Those working on excavations of mass graves, for instance, may work during most of the daylight hours and spend the evening planning the next day's activities. Those engaged in teaching may spend many hours in laboratory research or in preparing lessons to be taught. The work is interesting, however, and those employed in the field are usually highly motivated and unconcerned about long, irregular hours or primitive living conditions.

OUTLOOK

Overall, employment opportunities for anthropologists and archaeologists are expected to grow much faster than the average for all occupations through 2018, according to the U.S. Department of Labor. However, the fields of forensic anthropology and forensic archaeology are extremely small. As a result, while employment for professionals in these careers may be limited as a result of low turnover, advances in technology and testing procedures may create more opportunities for forensic anthropologists and archaeologists in the future as more agencies seek their skills to help solve cases.

Although college and university teaching has been the largest area of employment for all types of anthropologists and archaeologists, it will still be difficult to land a job in these highly competitive employment areas. Overall, the number of job applicants will be greater than the number of openings available. Competition will be great even for those with doctorates who are seeking faculty positions, and many will find only temporary or nontenured jobs.

FOR MORE INFORMATION

For information about forensic careers, education, and its membership section for physical anthropologists, contact
American Academy of Forensic Sciences
410 North 21st Street
Colorado Springs, CO 80904-2712
Tel: 719-636-1100
http://www.aafs.org

The following organization offers valuable information about anthropological careers and student associations:
American Anthropological Association
2200 Wilson Boulevard, Suite 600
Arlington, VA 22201-3357
Tel: 703-528-1902
http://www.aaanet.org

For information on graduate training in anthropology, contact
American Association of Physical Anthropologists
http://www.physanth.org

For information on certification, contact
American Board of Forensic Anthropology
http://www.theabfa.org

For information on forensic science, contact
American College of Forensic Examiners
2750 East Sunshine Street
Springfield, MO 65804-2047
Tel: 800-423-9737
http://www.acfei.com

For information on professional registration, contact
Register of Professional Archaeologists
5024-R Campbell Boulevard
Baltimore, MD 21236-5943

Tel: 410-933-3486
E-mail: info@rpanet.org
http://www.rpanet.org

For information on archaeological careers and job listings, contact
Society for American Archaeology
900 Second Street, NE, Suite 12
Washington, DC 20002-3560
Tel: 202-789-8200
E-mail: headquarters@saa.org
http://www.saa.org

The SAS is an association for "those interested in advancing our knowledge of the past through a wide range of techniques deriving from the fields of physics, chemistry, and the natural sciences." Visit its Web site for more information.
Society for Archaeological Sciences (SAS)
http://www.socarchsci.org

Geographic Information Systems Specialists

OVERVIEW

Geographic information systems (GIS) specialists create and analyze maps using sophisticated computer systems. GIS specialists in archaeology help archaeologists create maps of archaeological sites and their features (such as artifacts, rivers, vegetation, topography, and anything else that has a spatial component). They also help locate new archaeological sites. GIS specialists may have college degrees in archaeology, geographic information systems, geography, planning, engineering, or computer science.

HISTORY

Geographic information systems have grown up along with the rest of the computer industry in the past 30 to 35 years and have been pushed along particularly in the last 10 years by GIS software developers, extensive research and development, and widespread application of GIS in many different professional fields, including archaeology. In the past, archaeologists recorded various types of data on clear plastic sheets or thin graph paper that overlapped maps. This method could be confusing, time-consuming, and imprecise. GIS technology allows archaeologists to gather a large amount of information electronically. It allows them to obtain a larger understanding of a past culture and study it in multiple dimensions. GIS technology is even now being used on-site via handheld devices or software programs installed on notebooks and laptops.

THE JOB

GIS is basically a computer system that can assemble, store, manipulate, and display spatial data. GIS specialists in archaeology use this computer technology to combine digital mapmaking techniques with databases. GIS technology gives archaeologists the ability to map the components of a site, statistically analyze materials found at a site, view these components and materials in multiple dimensions, and generate new information and search strategies. The data are catalogued according to location or excavation level, stored in map form, and analyzed as though they were a map rather than a list. A GIS archaeology database might feature separate levels, or layers, for topography; vegetation; the location of artifacts, petroglyphs, structures, and graves; and almost any other type of information that can be presented spatially. Spatial information can be inputted from physical archaeological discoveries, site plans, existing maps, aerial photographs, satellite images, global positioning satellite data, and geophysical surveys. Exact coordinates are then created on the map; this process is called georeferencing.

GIS technology is used by archaeologists to answer many questions and solve problems. The following paragraphs provide just a few examples of its various uses.

Archaeologists and GIS specialists use GIS technology to analyze and compare data. For example, they can find out how many and what type of artifacts were found in a particular geographic area—such as areas above 5,000 feet or those found within 100 yards of a river—or in a particular type of site such as a village, cooking area, burial mound, or garbage pit. By finding similarities and differences between sites and artifacts, they can determine which cultures inhabited an area and when, among other findings.

Archaeologists in Peru are using GIS technology to record large-scale excavations to help understand how early cultures transitioned from a hunter-gatherer lifestyle to sedentary village life, understand the factors that caused local animals and plants to be domesticated, and document when these changes began to occur.

Archaeologists with the National Park Service have used GIS technology, photographs, old maps, and elevation data to locate lost sections of the Trail of Tears, a multistate route traversed by 16,000 Cherokee when they were forcibly removed by the U.S. Army from their ancestral lands in the 1830s.

In a cave in Belize, archaeologists have used GIS technology to map artifact placement for a planned archaeological museum. The site is unique because most of the artifacts are cemented to the floor as a result of a chemical process, which makes them difficult to remove (but still prone to damage). The site must be mapped so that archaeologists can track the condition and exact location of artifacts in order for them to be conserved and managed and exhibit areas can be built.

In Washington State, the Department of Archaeology and Historic Preservation and a GIS consulting firm created a GIS application that provided data on more than 19,000 archaeological sites and their contents (petroglyphs, burials, etc.) on land held by the state's 29 federally recognized tribes. The application was used by disaster responders and archaeologists after an oil spill, who were able to match areas affected by the spill with tribal lands—and contact the appropriate tribal government. Priceless resources were saved as a result of this technology. The National Park Service also has used GIS technology to save and protect archaeological resources after flooding in the Midwest and damage from Hurricane Katrina in New Orleans, among other areas.

GIS technology can also be used to create predictive models that help archaeologists locate new sites. Predictive models are created based on the concept that certain types of archaeological sites are found in similar geographic areas. For example, early cultures typically set up their camps within walking distance of a source of fresh water, but also sought the protection (against floods and enemies), when possible, of higher ground. After entering data about the topography and hydrology of a given areas into a GIS system, specialists can create a predictive model that indicates where similar undiscovered sites might be located. Or specialists using GIS technology might determine that many similar sites are located on or near a particular type of rock (perhaps one that was used for tool- or weapon-making), which would suggest that archaeologists should search for new sites that are located on or near similar rocks.

REQUIREMENTS
High School
To prepare for this career, take a college preparatory program while in high school. You will need a strong background in science (chemistry, physics, biology), mathematics (algebra, geometry, trigonometry, and calculus), graphic design, social studies, and especially computer science, so take as many of these classes as your school offers. In addition, take history classes, which will teach you about different

cultures. English courses will help you develop your research and writing skills. Also, consider taking a foreign language. This may help you fulfill some later college requirements as well as give you exposure to new words and place names and a sense of other cultures.

Postsecondary Training

You will need at least a bachelor's degree in GIS technology, geography, archaeology, planning, engineering, or computer science to work as a GIS specialist. More than 800 colleges and universities offer courses and programs in geographic information science. Visit the University Consortium for Geographic Information Science's Web site, http://www.ucgis.org/Membership/members.asp, for a list of member schools.

While not required, course work or a degree in archaeology or anthropology will provide excellent background experience for aspiring GIS specialists who want to work in archaeology. Conversely, some archaeologists earn certificates or degrees in GIS and specialize in this discipline.

GIS specialists must be proficient with GIS software. One of the most popular software programs for GIS specialists is ArcGIS. Some archaeology firms also hire GIS specialists to develop proprietary software for their specific needs. In this instance, a newly hired GIS specialist would learn how to use this software via on-the-job training.

Certification or Licensing

GIS specialists can receive voluntary certification from the GIS Certification Institute. Applicants must meet educational requirements based on a point system, complete course work and other documented education in GIS and geospatial data technologies, have work experience in a GIS-related position, and participate in conferences or GIS-related events. Applicants who meet all certification requirements may use the certified GIS professional designation.

Certification is also offered by the American Society for Photogrammetry and Remote Sensing.

Other Requirements

GIS specialists, naturally, must enjoy using computers and keeping up with technology developments that will affect their work, such as new software and new hardware. They should be detail oriented. Frequently, the projects GIS specialists work on are part of a team effort. These specialists, therefore, should be able to work well with others, meet deadlines, and clearly explain their findings. To keep up with their industry and advance in their jobs, GIS specialists must be committed to lifelong learning. GIS specialists who work in archaeology must be willing to travel to various sites and be away from home for extended periods of time, when necessary. GIS specialists also need skills in report writing, technical support, and teaching/training.

EXPLORING

Become comfortable with and read up on computers. There are books available on GIS technology and archaeology. Most are textbooks or geared toward professionals, but scanning them can provide you with a good overview of the field and GIS technology uses in archaeology. Two suggestions: *GIS and Archaeological Site Location Modeling,* by Mark W. Mehrer and Konnie L. Wescott (Boca Raton, Fla.: CRC Press, 2005) and *Geographical Information Systems in Archaeology,* by James Conolly and Mark Lake (New York: Cambridge University Press, 2006). You can also read GIS publications like the *Journal of GIS in Archaeology* (http://www.esri.com/industries/archaeology/business/journal.html), *GEO World* (http://www.geoplace.com), or *Geospatial Solutions* (http://www.gpsworld.com/gis).

Visiting Web sites and blogs about archaeology and GIS will also help you learn more. Here are a few suggestions: Computer Applications in Archaeology (http://www.u.arizona.edu/~mlittler), the Center for Advanced Spatial Technologies (http://cast.uark.edu), and GIS for Archaeology and CRM (http://www.gisarch.com).

If possible, visit an archaeology firm that provides or uses GIS services and ask questions. You might also ask your science teacher to arrange an information interview with a GIS specialist who works in archaeology.

EMPLOYERS

GIS specialists work for employers that provide GIS services to companies and organizations that conduct archaeological excavations. They are also employed directly by cultural resources management firms, museums, colleges and universities, salvage archaeology companies, and government agencies (such as state historic preservation offices, the National Park Service, U.S. Geological Survey, Bureau of Indian Affairs, and the Bureau of Land Management).

STARTING OUT

Look in GIS trade magazines for job opportunities or check with the career services office of your community college, college, or university. Search the Internet for sites that specialize exclusively in GIS employment opportunities.

Many archaeology and GIS professional associations and organizations offer job listings at their Web sites. Archaeology- and GIS-related employment sites that provide job listings include Earthworks-jobs.com (http://www.earthworks-jobs.com), eCulturalResources (http://www.eculturalresources.com/jobs.php), and GeoCommunity (http://careers.geocomm.com).

ADVANCEMENT

Advancement depends on the specific field and employer. Those working for a GIS company might rise from an analyst or software engineering position to manager, or move over to sales and marketing. Those employed in the field of archaeology advance by earning higher salaries, being assigned to larger projects, or being promoted to managerial positions. Some teach geographic information systems at colleges and universities.

EARNINGS

The U.S. Department of Labor (DOL) classifies the career of GIS specialist under the general category of cartographer. In 2009, median annual earnings for cartographers were $53,050. Salaries ranged from less than $32,520 to $90,410 or more. The DOL reports that cartographers employed by local government earned mean annual salaries of $53,960 and those working for the federal government earned mean annual salaries of $82,750.

In 2009, the American Cultural Resources Association conducted a survey of its members (including GIS specialists) to obtain information about salaries. It found that GIS specialists earned mean hourly salaries of $63 in 2008–09. Hourly wages ranged from $25 to $100.

Full-time GIS specialists usually receive benefits such as vacation days, sick leave, health and life insurance, and a savings and pension program. Self-employed specialists must provide their own benefits.

WORK ENVIRONMENT

GIS specialists typically work in office settings. Geographic information systems usually consist of PC-based workstations with big screens. (Some applications also are available for Macs, but the majority are for PCs.) In an organization where GIS is used extensively, each person might have a GIS workstation at his or her desk. GIS technology is also being used on-site at archaeological digs in the form of handheld computers combined with mobile GIS devices such as ArcPad or ArcView software operating on a laptop computer or a tablet personal computer.

OUTLOOK

The U.S. Department of Labor predicts that employment in the areas of surveying and mapping will grow faster than the average for all careers through 2018. The outlook for GIS specialists in archaeology is also strong. GIS technology is allowing archaeologists to quickly, but comprehensively, record and analyze information at archaeological sites. Opportunities should be best in the private sector—especially in cultural resources management.

FOR MORE INFORMATION

For industry information, contact
American Cultural Resources Association
5024-R Campbell Boulevard
Baltimore, MD 21236-5943
Tel: 410-933-3483
http://www.acra-crm.org

For information on careers in the field, contact
American Society for Photogrammetry and Remote Sensing
5410 Grosvenor Lane, Suite 210
Bethesda, MD 20814-2160
Tel: 301-493-0290
E-mail: asprs@asprs.org
http://www.asprs.org/career

For more information on careers in GIS and geography, visit the AAG Web site.
Association of American Geographers (AAG)
1710 16th Street, NW
Washington, DC 20009-3198
Tel: 202-234-1450
E-mail: gaia@aag.org
http://www.aag.org

Visit the society's Web site to read Cartography and GIS.
Cartography and Geographic Information Society
6 Montgomery Village Avenue, Suite 403
Gaithersburg, MD 20879-3557
Tel: 240-632-9716
http://www.cartogis.org

The institute offers an Archaeology User Community and publishes the Journal of GIS in Archaeology. *Visit its Web site for more information.*
Environmental Systems Research Institute
380 New York Street
Redlands, CA 92373-8100
Tel: 909-793-2853
http://www.esri.com
http://www.esri.com/industries/archaeology

For more information on certification, contact
GIS Certification Institute
701 Lee Street, Suite 680
Des Plaines, IL 60016-4539
Tel: 847-824-7768
E-mail: info@gisci.org
http://www.gisci.org

ESRI has created the site GIS.com, which provides information on topics such as what GIS is, GIS training, and GIS specialties.
GIS.com
http://www.gis.com

Visit the following NPS Web sites for information on national parks and other protected areas in the United States, GIS, careers, and volunteer opportunities, internships, and youth programs:
National Park Service (NPS)
U.S. Department of the Interior
Cultural Resources Geographic Information Systems Facility
1201 Eye Street, NW, 7th Floor (2270)
Washington, DC 20005-5905
Tel: 202-354-2135
E-mail: NPS_CRGIS@nps.gov
http://www.nps.gov
http://www.nps.gov/hdp/crgis

For information on archaeology careers and job listings, contact
Society for American Archaeology
900 Second Street, NE, Suite 12
Washington, DC 20002-3560
Tel: 202-789-8200
E-mail: headquarters@saa.org
http://www.saa.org

For career information, contact
Society for Historical Archaeology
9707 Key West Avenue, Suite 100
Rockville, MD 20850-3992
Tel: 301-990-2454
E-mail: hq@sha.org
http://www.sha.org
http://www.sha.org/EHA/splash.cfm

For information on educational programs in GIS technology, contact
University Consortium for Geographic Information Science
PO Box 15079
Alexandria, VA 22309-0079
Tel: 703-799-6698
http://ucgis.org

This science agency of the U.S. Department of the Interior has information on geospatial data, publications, education, and more on its Web site.
U.S. Geological Survey
National Center
12201 Sunrise Valley Drive
Reston, VA 20192-0002
Tel: 703-648-5953
http://www.usgs.gov

Government Archaeologists

QUICK FACTS

School Subjects
History
Speech

Personal Skills
Communication/ideas
Technical/scientific

Work Environment
Indoors and outdoors
Primarily multiple locations

Minimum Education Level
Master's degree

Salary Range
$31,530 to $71,400 to
$119,070+

Certification or Licensing
Voluntary

Outlook
Much faster than the average

DOT
054, 090

GOE
02.04.01, 12.03.02

NOC
4121, 4169

O*NET-SOC
19-3091.00, 19-3091.02,
25-1061.00

OVERVIEW

Archaeologists study the origin and evolution of humans. They study the physical evidence of human culture, examining such items as tools, burial sites, buildings, religious icons, pottery, and clothing. *Government archaeologists* are employed by local, state, and federal agencies that manage and protect cultural and natural resources, historic preservation offices, government-owned museums and cultural centers, and colleges and universities that are subsidized by the government.

HISTORY

Formal archaeological research in the United States began in 1784 when Thomas Jefferson directed the first scientific investigation of an ancient burial mound in Virginia. Scientific investigation, as well as what would be described today as looting, continued at our nation's archaeological sites—mainly Native American sites—throughout the late 1700s and 1800s as the young nation expanded West.

As the United States continued to grow, a large amount of land came under the control of the federal government, and early conservationists advocated for the creation of government agencies to oversee and protect these lands and their cultural and natural features. In 1849, the Department of the Interior was founded. Archaeologists were hired to investigate archaeological sites on these lands, but there was still no federal protection for the wealth of antiquities at these sites. In 1879, the Bureau of Ethnology was formed to conduct anthropological studies on the remaining Native American tribes that had not been decimated by illness or war. Anthropologists and archaeologists traveled throughout the country to conduct ethnographical studies of the tribes.

For the next 25 years, federal government land holdings increased and so did exploitation of archaeological resources. Massive looting occurred at many sites—especially in the American Southwest. Bills submitted by members of Congress to protect archaeological sites were not passed and only an executive order by President Benjamin Harrison allowed the Casa Grande Ruins in Arizona to become the first federal land to receive protection.

It was not until the passage of the Antiquities Act in 1906 that archaeological sites on federal land began to be protected. The act, according to the National Park Service, "decreed presidential authority to establish National Monuments and required permits to be approved before archaeological investigations could be undertaken on federal land." The enactment of the Antiquities Act marks the beginning of comprehensive fieldwork by archaeologists and protection of these resources. During the next 11 years the following national parks and monuments were established by Congress and American presidents: Devils Tower (Wyoming), El Morro (New Mexico), Montezuma Castle (Arizona), Chaco Canyon (New Mexico), Gila Cliff Dwellings (New Mexico), Tonto (Arizona), Tumacacori (Arizona), Gran Quivira (New Mexico), Navajo (Arizona), Big Hole Battlefield (Montana), Sitka (Alaska), Rainbow Bridge (Utah), Walnut Canyon (Arizona), and Bandelier (New Mexico). Nearly all of these parks and monuments had significant archaeological sites that required study, documentation, and conservation by archaeologists. In 1916, the National Park Service was founded to oversee these and other sites.

The Antiquities Act, combined with the passage of the Historic Sites Act of 1935, helped to launch an era in which more archaeological sites were protected. Federal government archaeologists stayed busy throughout the 1930s and 1940s in response to massive public works projects, including road building and the construction of dams and reservoirs. Archaeologists were needed to conduct site surveys and excavate and recover artifacts and remains before construction began.

In 1966, the National Historic Preservation Act mandated that the federal government should "provide leadership" for preservation, "contribute to" and "give maximum encouragement" to preservation, and "foster conditions under which our modern society and our prehistoric and historic resources can exist in productive harmony." This act also increased opportunities for archaeologists.

A heritage program manager for the U.S. Bureau of Land Management (*left*) joins other archaeology professionals in studying an excavation near Cochetopa Pass outside Saguache, Colorado. The excavation revealed three distinct fire sites and adds to evidence suggesting that the area served as either a camping ground or more permanent settlement for multiple groups of Native Americans through the centuries. *(Matt Hildner, AP Photo/*Pueblo Chieftain*)*

Today, government archaeologists continue to conduct fieldwork at national parks and monuments, in national forests, on other federal land, and at sites on state and local land. They also work at government-funded postsecondary institutions and museums as archaeologists, educators, and curators. Government archaeologists focus not only on prehistoric and historic Native American sites, but other archaeological sites ranging from Revolutionary War and Civil War battlefields, to sites of early trade and exploration, to the homes of historical figures, and any other site that is deemed important to our history.

THE JOB

Archaeologists who are employed by government agencies have a wide variety of duties and work in many different employment settings. The following paragraphs provide some examples of the work of government archaeologists.

Archaeologists who are employed by federal agencies such as the National Park Service (NPS), Bureau of Land Management, and U.S. Forest Service conduct archaeological research in laboratories and in the field at well-known locales (such as Mesa Verde National Park, Gettysburg National Military Park, Jamestown National Historic Site, and Chaco Culture National Historic Park) and lesser known, but no less interesting, sites (such as the Little Spanish Fort site in the Delta National Forest, Ebey's Landing National Historical Reserve, the Grant-Kohrs Ranch National Historic Site, the Knife River Indian Village National Historic Site, and the Mormon Pioneer National Historic Trail). Archaeologists also participate in inventories of archaeological resources at national parks and on other federal land to confirm the location of famous battles or other events, or to simply establish a record of archaeological sites so that they can be protected. One example of the former occurred at Sitka National Historic Park in Alaska. Archaeologists used metal detectors, other geophysical methods, and survey techniques to locate a fort that was built by Tlingit Indians in 1804 in preparation for battle with Russian colonists. The archaeologists recovered one-, two-, and 12-pound cannon balls and musket balls. Their location and other evidence confirmed the long-held anecdotal opinion of the location of the fort.

Federal agencies that manage public land must comply with the Native American Graves Protection and Repatriation Act (NAGPRA), which, according to the NPS "affirms the rights of Indian tribes, Native Alaskan entities, and Native Hawaiian organizations to custody of Native American human remains, funerary objects, sacred objects, and objects of cultural patrimony with which they have a relationship of cultural affiliation." Archaeologists conduct inventories of archaeological holdings to determine which artifacts and remains must be returned to Native American tribes under the act. This necessary, but time-consuming, process is ongoing, but as of 2009, more than 100 NPS units had completed NAGPRA inventories. The NPS reported that "nearly 6,000 sets of Native American human remains and over 82,000 associated funerary objects were listed in the inventories prepared and distributed to Indian tribes, Native Alaskan entities, and Native Hawaiian organizations."

Many archaeologists also work for state and local agencies that manage land or oversee archaeological and cultural resources on private land. Like archaeologists at the federal level, they conduct fieldwork at archaeological sites and spend a considerable portion of their time conducting research in laboratories. Each state in the United States has a *state archaeologist,* a highly trained archaeologist who is tasked with managing the state's archaeological resources. The state archaeologist manages an agency that is responsible for protecting and preserving archaeological sites; conducting research and laboratory analysis of artifacts and human remains; reviewing development plans so that archaeological sites are protected; providing information about archaeology and archaeological sites to the public; identifying and protecting human burial sites; licensing archaeological fieldwork; and enforcing archaeology-related laws.

Archaeologists employed at all government levels also conduct archaeological field surveys in advance of road construction, building projects, and leasing land to loggers in order to identify key sites. If sites are found, and the work is expected to damage the site, archaeologists carefully document and remove the artifacts for study, or they hire and supervise contract archaeologists to do the work. If a major site is found, roadwork or construction may be delayed or canceled in order to protect the resource. This type of work is called cultural resources management archaeology.

In addition to conducting fieldwork and research in laboratories, government archaeologists also write reports, articles, and books about their findings; serve as expert commentators on radio and television broadcasts; and participate in educational programs for the general public at visitor centers and in other settings.

Archaeologists also work as *teachers* at government-funded colleges and universities. They teach a variety of courses—ranging from entry-level classes such as Introduction to Archaeology and Archaeological Theory and Methods, to advanced courses in a particular specialty such as underwater archaeology or forensic archaeology. They participate in fieldwork and publish papers, articles, and books about their research.

Archaeologists can find employment at government-funded museums. These museums are stand-alone entities (such as the Smithsonian Institution National Museum of the American Indian) funded by governments at all levels or affiliated with government-funded universities and located on campuses. With additional training, they can work as *curators*. The primary duties of curators are maintenance, preservation, archiving, cataloguing, study, and display of collection components.

REQUIREMENTS

High School

Follow your high school's college prep program to prepare for undergraduate and graduate programs in archaeology. You should study English composition and literature to develop your writing and interpretation skills. Take classes in history and art to learn more about ancient and classical civilizations. Although it may seem that you'll be working mostly with ancient artifacts, you'll need computer skills to work with the many advanced technologies used in archaeological excavations. Mathematics and science courses can help you develop the skills you'll need in analyzing information and statistics.

Postsecondary Training

You will need at least a master's degree to work as a government archaeologist. Your first step on the path to earning a graduate degree is earning a bachelor's degree in archaeology, anthropology, history, historic preservation, or a related field. Archaeology departments are typically part of anthropology departments. There are few separate archaeology departments in U.S. colleges and universities. More than 350 colleges and universities have anthropology departments. While a student, it is also important to participate in internships and archaeological fieldwork. These activities are an excellent way to learn more about career options, and internships and fieldwork look impressive on a resume.

Certification or Licensing

The Register of Professional Archaeologists offers voluntary registration to archaeologists who agree to "abide by an explicit code of conduct and standards of research performance; who hold a graduate degree in archaeology, anthropology, art history, classics, history, or another germane discipline; and who have substantial practical experience."

Other Requirements

To succeed in archaeology, you need to be able to work well as part of a team and on your own. In order to be passionate about your study and research, you should be naturally curious and have a desire for knowledge. Communication skills are paramount, for writing reports, presenting your findings clearly and completely to professionals in the field, and interacting successfully with students (if you work as a teacher).

EXPLORING

To explore your interest in archaeology, read books about the field. Here are a few suggestions: *Archaeology For Dummies,* by Nancy Marie White (Hoboken, N.J.: For Dummies, 2008); *Archaeology Essentials: Theories, Methods and Practice,* by Paul Bahn and Colin Renfrew (London, U.K.: Thames & Hudson, 2007); and *Archaeology,* 5th ed., by Robert L. Kelly and David Hurst Thomas (Florence, Ky.: Wadsworth Publishing, 2009). Archaeology-related magazines provide a great overview of the field. You should also visit archaeology Web sites, especially those that are sponsored by government agencies. One suggestion: the National Park Service's Archaeology Program Web site, http://www.nps.gov/archeology.

A trip to a museum also will introduce you to the world of archaeology. Better yet, see if your local museum offers part-time work or volunteer opportunities. There are also many opportunities to volunteer with federal agencies. Information on volunteer opportunities with the Bureau of Land Management, Fish & Wildlife Service, U.S. Forest Service, National Park Service, U.S. Army Corps of Engineers, Bureau of Indian Affairs, and U.S. Geological Survey can be found at http://www.volunteer.gov/gov. Additionally, you can participate in the federal government's Student Educational Employment Program (SEEP). High school students in SEEP are employed in entry-level positions with federal agencies that match their interests and career goals. Applicants must be U.S. citizens or residents of American Samoa or Swains Islands. Successful completion of SEEP may lead to permanent opportunities in federal service upon completion of other educational requirements (namely, a college degree). College students at the undergraduate and graduate levels are also eligible to participate in SEEP. For further information, visit http://www.opm.gov/employ/students.

The U.S. Forest Service offers Passport in Time, a "volunteer archaeology and historic preservation program . . . where volunteers work with professional Forest Service archaeologists and historians on national forests throughout the U.S. on such diverse activities as archaeological survey and excavation, rock art restoration, survey, archival research, historic structure restoration, oral history gathering, and analysis and curation of artifacts." Visit http://www.passportintime.com for more information.

If you want to become an archaeology professor, talk to your teachers about what it is like to be an educator. Perhaps you could even arrange an information interview with an archaeologist or an archaeology professor.

EMPLOYERS

Government archaeologists in the United States are employed by local, state, and federal agencies that manage and protect cultural and natural resources, government-owned museums and cultural centers (such as the Smithsonian Institution National Museum of the American Indian), state and local archaeology and historic preservation offices, and colleges and universities that are subsidized by the government. Major federal government employers of archaeologists include the National Park Service, U.S. Forestry Service, the Bureau of Land Management, U.S. Fish and Wildlife Service, and U.S. Army Corps of Engineers. Archaeologists also work for highway departments, parks departments, and water resource departments.

STARTING OUT

You may have an opportunity to work as a research assistant or a teaching fellow while in graduate school, and frequently this experience is of tremendous help in qualifying for your first job. Your graduate school professors should be able to help you establish contacts in the field.

While in school, you should also be involved in internships to gain experience. Internship opportunities may be available through your graduate program, or you may have to seek them out yourself. You can check with your state's archaeological society or government agencies to find out about volunteer opportunities.

To learn more about opportunities with the federal government, contact your local Federal Job Information Center or the federal Office of Personnel Management (http://www.usajobs.gov) for application information. Information on jobs at the state and local level is available at state employment offices and their Web sites and by directly contacting government-funded historic preservation offices, museums, and colleges and universities.

ADVANCEMENT

Government archaeologists advance by receiving higher pay or being assigned managerial duties. The normal pattern of advancement for archaeology teachers is from instructor to assistant professor, to associate professor, to full professor. All four academic ranks are concerned primarily with teaching and research. Archaeologists also advance by becoming renowned for their work, writing books and articles about their findings, appearing as experts on radio and television broadcasts, and pursuing opportunities in the private sector, which often pay higher salaries than government employers.

EARNINGS

The U.S. Department of Labor (DOL) reports that mean annual earnings for archaeologists employed by the federal government were $71,400 in 2009. Those employed by local and state governments earned $55,500 and $50,290, respectively. Salaries for all archaeologists ranged from less than $31,530 to $87,890 or more.

According to the DOL, postsecondary anthropology and archaeology teachers employed at both public and private institutions earned median annual salaries of $69,520 in 2009, with 10 percent earning $119,070 or more and 10 percent earning $41,270 or less.

Benefits for full-time workers include paid vacation, health, disability, life insurance, and retirement or pension plans.

WORK ENVIRONMENT

Archaeologists working in educational facilities and offices have normally clean, well-lit, and ventilated environments. Those working in the field may work in a tougher environment, working in all types of weather and, depending on the area to which they are assigned, they may deal with potentially difficult living conditions.

Archaeologists work about 40 hours a week, and the hours may be irregular. Physical strength and stamina is necessary for fieldwork of all types. Those working on excavations, for instance, may work during most of the daylight hours and spend the evening planning the next day's activities. Excavation work may be tough, but most find the work interesting and well worth the irregular hours or primitive living conditions.

OUTLOOK

The U.S. Department of Labor predicts that employment for all archaeologists will grow much faster than the average for all occupations through 2018. In recent years, government funding for cultural and natural resources protection has been reduced. Funding for federal agencies that oversee the protection of cultural, archaeological, and natural resources is expected to increase somewhat under the Obama administration. Despite this prediction, it is important to remember that there are only a small number of government archaeologists. Competition is strong for these positions. Archaeologists with advanced degrees and experience in the field will have the best opportunities.

Although overall employment for college professors is expected to grow faster than the average for all careers through 2018, employment for anthropology and archaeology educators will not be as strong. Again, this is a small field and competition for tenure-track positions is high.

FOR MORE INFORMATION

For information on careers, education and training, and internships for museum professionals, contact
American Association of Museums
1575 Eye Street, NW, Suite 400

Washington, DC 20005-1113
Tel: 202-289-1818
http://www.aam-us.org

*To read about the issues affecting college professors, contact the
following organizations:*
American Association of University Professors
1133 19th Street, NW, Suite 200
Washington, DC 20036-3655
Tel: 202-737-5900
E-mail: aaup@aaup.org
http://www.aaup.org

American Federation of Teachers
555 New Jersey Avenue, NW
Washington, DC 20001-2029
Tel: 202-879-4400
http://www.aft.org

*Visit the BLM Web site for information on its land holdings and
career and volunteer opportunities.*
Bureau of Land Management (BLM)
U.S. Department of the Interior
1849 C Street, Room 5665
Washington, DC 20240-0001
Tel: 202-208-3801
http://www.blm.gov

*For an overview of the career of archaeologist written by an associ-
ate professor of anthropology, visit*
**Frequently Asked Questions About a Career in Archaeology in
the U.S.**
http://www.museum.state.il.us/ismdepts/anthro/dlcfaq.html

*For information on state archaeologists and archaeology museums
and resources, contact*
National Association of State Archaeologists
http://www.uiowa.edu/~osa/nasa

*Visit the NPS Web site for information on national parks and other
protected areas in the United States, careers, and volunteer opportunities, internships, and youth programs.*
National Park Service (NPS)
U.S. Department of the Interior

1849 C Street, NW
Washington, DC 20240-0001
Tel: 202-208-3818
http://www.nps.gov

For information on professional registration, contact
Register of Professional Archaeologists
5024-R Campbell Boulevard
Baltimore, MD 21236-5943
Tel: 410-933-3486
E-mail: info@rpanet.org
http://www.rpanet.org

For information on archaeological careers and job listings, contact
Society for American Archaeology
900 Second Street, NE, Suite 12
Washington, DC 20002-3560
Tel: 202-789-8200
E-mail: headquarters@saa.org
http://www.saa.org

*The SAS is an association for "those interested in advancing our
knowledge of the past through a wide range of techniques deriving
from the fields of physics, chemistry, and the natural sciences." Visit
its Web site for more information.*
Society for Archaeological Sciences (SAS)
http://www.socarchsci.org

For career information, contact
Society for Historical Archaeology
9707 Key West Avenue, Suite 100
Rockville, MD 20850-3992
Tel: 301-990-2454
E-mail: hq@sha.org
http://www.sha.org
http://www.sha.org/EHA/splash.cfm

For information on career opportunities, contact
U.S. Army Corps of Engineers
441 G. Street, NW
Washington, DC 20314-1000
Tel: 202-761-0011
E-mail: hq-publicaffairs@usace.army.mil
http://www.usace.army.mil

The U.S. Fish and Wildlife Service manages the 96-million-acre National Wildlife Refuge System. This system includes 548 National Wildlife Refuges, thousands of smaller wetlands, and other special management areas. Visit its Web site for information on archaeology careers, conservation, endangered species, and volunteer opportunities.

U.S. Fish and Wildlife Service
4401 North Fairfax Drive, Mailstop: 330
Arlington, VA 22203-1610
Tel: 703-358-1780
http://www.fws.gov

For information about careers and information on national forests across the country, contact

U.S. Forest Service
U.S. Department of Agriculture
Attn: Office of Communication
Mailstop: 1111
1400 Independence Avenue, SW
Washington, DC 20250-1111
Tel: 800-832-1355
E-mail: info@fs.fed.us
http://www.fs.fed.us

INTERVIEW

Scott Anfinson is the state archaeologist for Minnesota. He discussed the field and his career with the editors of Careers in Focus: Archaeology.

Q. What is one thing that young people may not know about a career in archaeology?

A. Popular views of archaeology are highly romanticized. Most American archaeologists will never dig a Greek temple or even go to Egypt. The great majority of archaeologists worldwide are involved in what is known as "heritage management." This is an outgrowth of environmental protection laws and mainly involves limiting harm to archaeological sites from development projects. Surveys are done to find sites, the sites are evaluated for importance, and then the important sites are usually avoided. Modern archaeology involves less fieldwork and more paperwork.

Q. How long have you worked in the field? What made you want to enter the field?

A. I have worked in archaeology for more than 30 years, mainly in Minnesota. My interest in archaeology started with a fascination in the ancient past. It began with dinosaurs (paleontology), moved to Classical Mediterranean archaeology, and eventually settled on prehistoric North American archaeology.

Q. How did you train for this career?

A. There are three basic archaeological career paths in North American universities: prehistoric archaeology, historical archaeology, or classical archaeology. Prehistoric archaeologists come out of anthropology departments; historical archaeologists come out of history, anthropology, or specialized historical archaeology departments; and classical archaeologists come out of classics departments. To be a low-level fieldworker, you usually need a bachelor's degree and field school experience. To be a supervisor in heritage management, you need a master's degree. To teach at a university, you need a doctoral degree. I have all three degrees and all three are in anthropology with a specialty in archaeology.

Q. Can you please describe a day in your life on the job. What are your typical work responsibilities?

A. I am currently the state archaeologist for Minnesota. My responsibilities include licensing archaeologists to work on public land, reviewing development plans to help reduce impacts to important archaeological sites, working with Indian leaders to help preserve burial sites, providing leadership for promoting archaeological research, and being the major archaeological interface with the general public. I spend a lot of time talking to archaeologists, Indians, officials, and the public. My office is in a historical interpretive center at Fort Snelling. Here we have records of all the known archaeological sites in the state, laboratories for artifact analysis, and offices for a number of archaeologists who work for me or for other programs. I also teach archaeology at the University of Minnesota, which gives me a chance to work with students and share what I have learned over the last 30 years.

Q. What are the most important personal and professional qualities for archaeologists?

A. Archaeologists must be problem solvers. Understanding the past is a problem to be solved. We use both scientific and historical methods to solve problems. Once a problem is solved or even if we don't solve it, we must let others know about our work. If knowledge is not passed on, it is worthless. Therefore archaeologists must be good writers. If I had to pick one skill that can be learned in high school that will serve an archaeologist well, I would pick writing. Math and computer skills are also important. High-level archaeologists must first and foremost be good writers.

Q. What are some of the pros and cons of your job?
A. I enjoy traveling and working with people. These can be pros or cons, as too much traveling is very tiring and some people can be overly demanding. Most of all I enjoy solving mysteries and no job is better than archaeology for providing mysteries to be solved. We have a million years of mysteries that need solving. Because I am a state official, I have limited time to actually do archaeology because I must be available to agencies, elected officials, and the public. Most of all, I enjoy doing my job. That is much more important than money or fame.

Historians

QUICK FACTS

School Subjects
Foreign language
Geography
History

Personal Skills
Communication/ideas
Helping/teaching

Work Environment
Primarily indoors
Primarily multiple locations

Minimum Education Level
Master's degree

Salary Range
$25,850 to $51,050 to
$110,570+

Certification or Licensing
Required (for secondary
school teachers)

Outlook
About as fast as the average

DOT
052

GOE
02.04.02

NOC
4169

O*NET-SOC
19-3093.00, 25-1125.00

OVERVIEW

Historians study, assess, and interpret the activities and conduct of individuals or social, ethnic, political, or geographical groups of the past.

HISTORY

Throughout the history of civilization some people have either recorded or passed along orally the significant events and ideas of their times. People in ancient Egypt, Greece, and Rome wrote accounts of the life and events of those great civilizations. In fact, the Greek writer Herodotus generally is considered the first historian. Historical writings help us to know the people and leaders who lived centuries ago and how their actions may have influenced the development of modern civilization. It is the job of historians to analyze the past and present us with this information. Often, we can make better decisions and plan more carefully for the future if we are aware of the actions, judgments, precedents, and mistakes of the past.

Much of our knowledge of history had been gleaned by modern professional historians who have studied manuscripts, documents, artifacts, and other traces of earlier periods. Some of the manuscripts or writings they study were written as actual historical accounts; others may be letters, diaries, or fiction with some historical basis.

THE JOB

Modern historians are trained to gather, interpret, and evaluate the records of the past in order to describe and analyze past events, institutions, ideas, and people. Skill in research and writing is essential to their work, but scientific methods are also invaluable.

Some historians are college teachers; others write books and articles, do research, and lecture. Historians work for museums, special libraries, and historical societies, and they are often called on as advisers in such fields as politics, economics, law, and education. They also research the accuracy of historical details in stage, motion picture, and TV presentations. Most specialize in the history of a specific country or region or a specific period or industry. A historian may choose to become an expert in ancient, medieval, or modern times, They may also choose to specialize in specific topics such as Native American tribes of the Northwest, British law, World War II, or the Civil Rights Movement.

Some historians research the accuracy of historical details in stage, motion picture, television, and radio presentations. They authenticate such things as customs, speech, costumes, architectural styles, modes of transportation, and other items peculiar to a particular period of history. The research department of a film or television production company may be headed by a *research director.*

Historians who are called *archivists* are responsible for identifying, preserving, and cataloging historical documents of value to writing, researching, or teaching history. They are really history librarians who have learned the technique of selectivity; that is, they recognize which historical materials are worth preserving, since it would be impossible to save all material. Such historians may work in museums, libraries, historical societies, and also for the U.S. government, where they may collect materials, write about the activities of various departments, and prepare pamphlets, lectures, exhibits, or presentations on the Internet.

Curators work for a museum, special library, or historical society. They identify and preserve historical documents and other articles of the past such as clothing, pottery, artwork, and other items that have been preserved through time or discovered via archaeological fieldwork. Often curators help scholars with research in the institution's collection. *Historical society directors* are curators who coordinate the activities of a historical society. They direct the research staff, review publications and exhibits, speak before various groups and organizations, and perform the administrative duties involved in running a historical institution.

Genealogists specialize in family histories. They use public records, such as birth and death certificates, military records, census studies, and real estate deeds, to trace connections between individuals. If they are researching the history of a notable family, they may even work with archaeologists who have conducted field research or excavations at family estates, businesses, or other properties owned by the family. They are like detectives in a sense, but they must have the patience to continue following up leads in one historical record after another.

REQUIREMENTS

High School
If you are interested in becoming a historian, be sure to take college-preparatory courses in high school. Historians must be strong readers, writers, and speakers, so a strong background in English and speech will prepare you for further study in college. A knowledge of at least two foreign languages is also necessary for those who plan to earn a doctorate.

Postsecondary Training
The main educational requirement for a historian is graduate study. A master's degree in history is the minimum requirement for a college instructor's position, but the doctorate is much more desirable and is required by many colleges and universities. To become a professor or administrator, or to reach any other high level of employment, a doctorate is essential. Historians working for museums, historical societies, research councils, or the federal government generally have doctorates or the equivalent in training and experience. A person is rarely considered a professional historian without this educational background. The American Historical Association offers a list of doctoral programs in history at its Web site, http://www.historians.org.

Some jobs for beginners with a bachelor's degree in history are available, usually with federal, state, or local governments. These jobs usually require a knowledge of the archivist's work, but advancement without further education is unlikely. A number of high school teaching positions are also available, provided the applicant meets state requirements for certification.

Certification or Licensing
Historians who work as public school teachers must be licensed under regulations established by the department of education of the state in which they teach. Not all states require licensure for teachers in private or parochial schools. Contact your state's department of education for more information.

Other Requirements
To be a successful historian, you should have a real love for history and the past especially as you work long hours in research and writ-

ing. Historians need to have analytical minds capable of sifting facts scientifically. You must also be dedicated, self-motivated, and curious about the world around you. If you choose to become a history teacher, you should have good speaking skills, patience, and enjoy working with students.

EXPLORING

Reading about history is a great way to find out if this career is for you. You might want to pick up a copy of *Careers for Students of History,* which is published by the American Historical Association (AHA), the National Council on Public History, and the Public History Program at the University of South Carolina. The book profiles history-related careers in education, museums and archives, publishing, historic preservation, government, and consulting. To learn more about this book, visit the AHA Web site, http://www. historians.org.

You can also learn a great deal about a career as a historian by talking to your history teachers or arranging interviews with historians working in local museums or universities. You can experiment with research in the field of history by developing your own history projects, such as tracing the genealogy of your family or researching the history of your neighborhood or town. By seeking the advice of your history teacher while working on these projects, you will get a good feel for doing real research and drawing conclusions based on the historical information you have discovered.

EMPLOYERS

A large percentage of historians are employed at colleges and universities, while others teach at the middle or high school level. Historians are also employed in archives, historical societies, libraries, museums, non-profit foundations, research councils, and large corporations. Others work for local, state, and the federal government. Historians employed by the federal government often work at the National Archives and the Departments of Defense, Interior, and State. Some historians work in politics or journalism or serve as consultants to radio, television, or film producers.

STARTING OUT

Historians interested in becoming teachers enter the field after completing at least a master's degree in history. At this time, they may apply for an instructor's position at a college or university or

142　Careers in Focus: Archaeology

they may seek employment as a history teacher at a middle school or high school.

Historians who are interested in nonacademic positions may learn about job leads through internships, professors, or from the career services office of their college or university. The American Historical Association also offers job listings to its student and professional members at its Web site. Many historians earn a doctorate before applying for nonteaching positions.

ADVANCEMENT

Historians advance in proportion to their level of education, experience, and personal skills as writers, researchers, or teachers. University teachers usually begin as instructors. The next step is assistant professor, then associate professor, and finally full rank as a professor.

Historians in noneducational settings advance as they gain experience and contribute to their work. Historians who have earned a doctorate already have a competitive edge over workers with lesser degrees and, therefore, enjoy stronger advancement opportunities.

EARNINGS

The U.S. Department of Labor (DOL) reports that historians earned average annual salaries of $51,050 in 2009. Salaries ranged from less than $25,850 to $95,750 or more annually. The DOL reports that historians earned the following mean annual salaries by employer: management, scientific, and technical consulting services, $73,420; museums, historical sites, and similar institutions, $48,490; scientific research and development services, $46,740; and local government, $36,770.

College history teachers earned salaries that ranged from less than $35,510 to more than $110,570 in 2009. History teachers employed at four-year universities earned higher mean salaries ($71,220 annually) than history teachers employed by junior colleges ($64,460 annually).

Historians and history teachers often receive benefits such as medical insurance, paid sick and vacation days, and the opportunity to participate in retirement savings plans.

WORK ENVIRONMENT

Historians employed in educational settings will enjoy clean, well-lighted, and pleasant work settings. College and university professors may have their own offices, or they may have to share an office with one or more colleagues. College professors enjoy a flexible schedule that allows them to arrange their schedule around class hours, academic meetings, and the established office hours when they meet with students. Although history professors may teach only two or three classes a semester, they spend a considerable amount of time preparing for lectures, examining student work, and conducting research.

Historians who teach at the middle- or high-school level will have more traditional hours. They may also be required to teach others types of classes and supervise extracurricular activities as part of their duties.

Historians who are employed in noneducational settings usually work in professional office settings. They may have to spend long hours in library stacks or searching electronic databases for the tiniest piece of information. Historians may be required to travel to conduct interviews or gather information at archives, museums, or other locations.

OUTLOOK

The *Occupational Outlook Handbook* reports that employment for historians is expected to grow about as fast as the average for all occupations through 2018. Historians who are employed in policy and research and historic preservation will have the best employment opportunities in the next decade. The employment outlook at colleges and universities is not as promising. Competition for college faculty positions is so keen that many historians with doctorates have to accept part-time positions or find work in other occupations. Historians holding only master's degrees will also face much competition.

FOR MORE INFORMATION

For general information on the study of history, contact
American Association for State and Local History
1717 Church Street
Nashville, TN 37203-2991
Tel: 615-320-3203
http://www.aaslh.org

For information on teaching careers at the university level, contact
American Association of University Professors
1133 19th Street, NW, Suite 200
Washington, DC 20036-3655

Tel: 202-737-5900
E-mail: aaup@aaup.org
http://www.aaup.org

For comprehensive information on careers and educational opportunities, contact
American Historical Association
400 A Street, SE
Washington, DC 20003-3889
Tel: 202-544-2422
E-mail: info@historians.org
http://www.historians.org

The following Web site was designed for high school and college teachers of U.S. history courses. It has a variety of interesting information and links.
History Matters: The U.S. Survey Course on the Web
http://www.historymatters.gmu.edu

For information about history education, contact
National Council for History Education
7100 Baltimore Avenue, Suite 510
College Park, MD 20740-3641
Tel: 440-835-1776
E-mail: nche@nche.net
http://www.nche.net

The National History Center is "dedicated to the study and teaching of history, as well as to the advancement of historical knowledge in government, business, and the public at large." Visit its Web site for more information.
The National History Center
400 A Street, SE
Washington, DC 20003-3889
Tel: 202-544-2422, ext. 103
http://nationalhistorycenter.org

For information about student membership and job listings, contact
Organization of American Historians
112 North Bryan Avenue
Bloomington, IN 47408-4141
Tel: 812-855-7311
http://www.oah.org

Historic Preservationists

OVERVIEW

Historic preservationists are champions of buildings and sites of historic or cultural significance. Their duties include the identification, evaluation, protection, and renovation of archaeological sites, parks, structures, buildings, or entire neighborhoods. They may also help manage ongoing maintenance of restored structures or sites.

HISTORY

Many historians agree the first major restoration project documented in the United States was Mount Vernon, the home of George Washington, the first president of the United States. In 1889, a group of women concerned about the state of President Washington's home, formed the Mount Vernon's Ladies Association and restored the mansion and grounds to its former glory.

Also in 1889, the Association of the Preservation of Virginia's Antiquities became the first statewide historic group in the United States. The organization, now known as APVA Preservation Virginia, owns and maintains various historically important sites throughout the state of Virginia.

The biggest boost to the preservation movement was the passage of the 1966 National Historic Preservation Act. The law reinforced the government's commitment to caring for the nation's historic treasures. From then on, defining, restoring, and maintaining sites and structures were done according to a certain standard.

QUICK FACTS

School Subjects
Art
History

Personal Skills
Artistic
Helping/teaching

Work Environment
Indoors and outdoors
Primarily multiple
  locations

Minimum Education Level
Bachelor's degree

Salary Range
$25,850 to $51,050 to
  $95,750+

Certification or Licensing
None available

Outlook
About as fast as the average

DOT
052

GOE
02.04.02

NOC
4169

O*NET-SOC
19-3093.00

The National Park Service (NPS) is a federal bureau of the U.S. Department of the Interior responsible for resources owned by the government, such as archeological sites, battlefields, natural landscapes, monuments, and historical homes. The NPS also sets regulations under which privately owned historical districts are managed. The NPS administers many agencies devoted to cultural and historical resources. One agency, the National Register of Historic Places, identifies and protects districts, sites, homes, and objects that are relevant to the culture or history of the United States. Once listed in the National Register, a home or site is protected from future demolition, and may be eligible for federal funding to be used for renovation or promotion.

THE JOB

The industry of historic preservation received a tremendous boost with the passage of the 1966 National Historic Preservation Act—which gave direction and focus toward the U.S. government's commitment to better care for its historic resources. This law created a need for qualified historians and historic preservationists well trained to identify, preserve, and maintain our national treasures.

Today, historic preservationists can find employment in a variety of settings. Many employed by the federal government work for the NPS. Examples of various NPS areas managed by historic preservationists include battlefields, such as Spotsylvania in Virginia and the Little Bighorn Battlefield National Monument in Montana; historic sites in national parks and at other NPS sites (such as the Old Faithful Inn at Yellowstone National Park, the Knife River Indian Villages National Historic Site in North Dakota, and the Charles Pinckney National Historic Site in South Carolina, where African American slaves once lived), and other places of interest such as Mount Rushmore. Their responsibilities may include researching the site's origin, implementing plans of routine maintenance and preservation, and suggesting marketing and educational campaigns to present the site to the public. For example, historic preservationists may suggest plans to help retard erosion in a famous battlefield or educate the public about the childhood home of a former president. They may also conduct research on architectural styles and period-specific décor to properly restore, for example, one of Abraham Lincoln's childhood homes, to its former condition. Many times a museum is housed alongside a historic site or national park to further educate the public regarding its significance. Preservationists are often employed to help plan the scope of a museum's exhibits and design an educational program for visitors of all ages.

Historic preservationists may also work at the state level. As a result of the 1966 National Preservation Act, each state is required to maintain an office that acts as a liaison for federal and local preservation agencies. State-employed historic preservationists conduct inventories of structures and sites of historic importance, prepare educational programs, and investigate possible National Register nominations. State historical offices are often considered a resource for communities or individuals who may have a particular building or site with historic or cultural relevance. For example, if a landowner suspected that Native American burial mounds or the remains of a 17th- century French fort were present on his property, he would contact his state's historic office. Preservationists would then verify the site's significance, and begin the paperwork needed to register the site as a national or state landmark.

Historic preservationists may also work at the local level. Many cities and towns maintain planning commissions or economic development offices to help preserve historic sites or artistic styles within their own communities. For example, when a town experiences a large growth spurt or undergoes a major downtown renovation, planning commissions, alongside historic preservationists, want to ensure that growth is monitored, without comprising a neighborhood's important architectural elements or historical or cultural significance. Local volunteers may make up the majority of the staff, but a qualified preservationist is often retained full time to conduct research, create educational programs and tours, and ensure that existing and potential historic sites are maintained within local regulations. Preservationists may also take on many other duties such a clerical work, conducting tours, or any other tasks needed to get a project off the ground.

Historic preservationists may also find employment at private firms as full-time employees at larger organizations, or at smaller companies as part-time employees or consultants. At this level, preservationists use their training to promote awareness of a community's historical treasures of architecture, art, archaeological, or natural resource, find sufficient funding from public and/or private sources, and maintain a project within a designated budget.

REQUIREMENTS

High School

Your love of history is a good foundation for a career in preservation. In high school, take as many history classes as possible. Start with U.S. history, but also consider the history of art and architecture. Business classes such as marketing and finance will prove helpful when raising funding for a new project, or finishing one within a set budget. As a historic preservationist, you will be expected to write proposals to nominate a potential site, research a specific architectural style, or work as a liaison between federal and local agencies. Begin your training with classes that will strengthen your writing and speaking skills such as speech and English.

Postsecondary Training

More than 55 colleges and universities throughout the United States offer undergraduate or graduate degrees in historic preservation. You'll want to make sure your program of choice is listed with the National Council for Preservation Education (http://www.ncpe.us/chart.html), which closely monitors programs specializing in this discipline. Most positions, especially those connected with the federal government, require at least a bachelor's degree. Management positions, such as those of staff historian, will require a master's degree or Ph.D.

Expect to take classes that focus on the history of a particular design, such as architecture, landscape, archaeology, or urban development. You will also take classes on the proper techniques of preservation and documentation. Many programs also offer elective classes in law, real estate development, business, government, and design.

Most programs also require successful completion of an internship or apprenticeship. For example, if you choose to intern at the National Park Service you could acquire valuable field experience working alongside professionals at a variety of locations—a historic site, museum, or national landmark.

Other Requirements

Historical preservationists work on many types of projects, from large government-funded restorations of a city devastated by natural disaster, to archaeological restorations at state and national parks, to small grassroots campaign to save a town's Main Street. In turn, preservation professionals must be able to deal with all types of people—from federal officials to ordinary citizens. They must be ready to interpret their research into terms easily understood by those outside of the field.

Preservationists must be meticulous with their work, often spending many hours on research, fieldwork, or lobbying various government agencies. Organization and patience are skills highly valued in this industry.

EXPLORING

Would you like to learn more about the field of historic preservation? You can begin by contacting your local historical society; most towns maintain such an office dedicated to preserving sites and structures within the community. You may be asked to volunteer for a number of tasks ranging from clerical—answering phones, paperwork, mass mailings—to ones that provide you with hands-on experience such as conducting tours of a historical home to gathering signatures for a landmark petition.

Pass on that vacation to a seaside resort and opt instead for a driving tour of the nation's best landmarks. Don't forget to visit museums or tourist centers often located near the sites to learn more about the structure or landmark. Visit the National Trust's Web site (http://www.nationaltrust.org) for its annual list of the country's best destinations and treasures, as well as a list of those that are endangered.

EMPLOYERS

The government comprises the largest source of employment for historic preservationists, the majority of which fall under the auspices of the National Park Service. The NPS monitors the work of division offices such as the National Register of Historic Places, the National Historic Landmarks Program, and the Historic American Buildings Survey. Other employment opportunities exist with state and local government agencies, private consulting firms, and nonprofit groups.

STARTING OUT

A college education is required for most jobs in preservation, but work experience is highly valued as well. Most graduates begin their career during an internship as a research assistant for a restoration site or archaeology project. Other entry-level jobs at the NPS, for example, include researchers and writers for various educational programs for museums and schools, industry journals, and publications written for the general public.

ADVANCEMENT

Career advancement can be achieved with relevant work experience and additional training. Many preservationists move on to work or manage larger projects within their specific expertise or special interest.

Experienced preservationists may also advance to positions in the private sector. Many businesses, such as architectural firms or law firms specializing in the housing market, may not be interested in restoration, but still desire skilled professionals with knowledge of the National Register. Some preservationists, especially those interested in the legal side of restoration, opt to pursue a law degree specializing in restoration law. Some law schools offer a dual degree in law and a preservation-related field such as urban planning.

EARNINGS

The U.S. Department of Labor does not provide salary information for historic preservationists, but it does report that *historians,* professionals that perform work that is often similar to that of preservationists, earned average annual salaries of $51,050 in 2009. Salaries ranged from less than $25,850 to $95,750 or more annually.

Historical preservationists typically receive benefits such as medical insurance, paid sick and vacation days, and the opportunity to participate in retirement savings plans.

WORK ENVIRONMENT

Most historic preservationists work in professional office settings, although some have offices at historical sites. They may be required to travel to inspect or gather information at historic sites and other locations. Most preservationists work a standard 40-hour week, but they may have to work evenings and weekends to attend public hearings with citizens' groups or meet with other professionals in the field.

OUTLOOK

Cities and towns are beginning to recognize the financial, cultural, and historical importance of buildings, structures, archaeological sites, natural areas, and other places. As a result, there is an increasing need for historic preservationists. Despite this growth, funding for historic preservation is largely tied to the health of the economy. When the economy is strong, private organizations and government agencies can allot more funds to historical preservation projects. When the economy is weak, there are fewer funds available, and preservation projects, and even employment for historic preservationists, may be limited. As always, those with the most experience and training will have the best employment prospects.

FOR MORE INFORMATION

For a list of schools granting degrees in historic preservation and available internships, contact
   National Council for Preservation Education
   E-mail: info@ncpe.us
   http://www.ncpe.us

The National Park Service is the umbrella agency for numerous offices devoted to the preservation of historic places. For a list of all federal offices and their liaisons, job opportunities, and available internships, contact

National Park Service
1849 C Street, NW
Washington, DC 20240-0001
Tel: 202-208-6843
http://www.nps.gov
http://www.nps.gov/history/archeology

For continuing education opportunities and seminars, contact

National Preservation Institute
PO Box 1702
Alexandria, VA 22313-1702
Tel: 703-765-0100
E-mail: info@npi.org
http://www.npi.org

For career and educational opportunities in historic preservation, information on advocacy groups and forums, internship possibilities, and to obtain a copy of its bimonthly magazine, Preservation, *contact*

National Trust for Historic Preservation
1785 Massachusetts Avenue, NW
Washington, DC 20036-2117
Tel: 202-588-6040
http://www.preservationnation.org

Laboratory Testing
Technicians

QUICK FACTS

School Subjects
Chemistry
History
Physics

Personal Skills
Following instructions
Technical/scientific

Work Environment
Indoors and outdoors
One location with some travel

Minimum Education Level
Associate's degree

Salary Range
$25,540 to $53,240 to
$96,110+

Certification or Licensing
None available (certification)
Required by certain states
(licensing)

Outlook
About as fast as the average

DOT
029

GOE
2.05.01, 02.05.02

NOC
2211, 2212

O*NET-SOC
19-4021.00, 19-4031.00,
19-4041.00, 19-4092.00,
19-4099.00

OVERVIEW

Laboratory testing technicians who work in the field of archaeology conduct tests on artifacts and human and animal remains. They work in laboratories and in the field at archaeological digs.

HISTORY

In the early days of archaeology, archaeologists conducted most of the testing of the artifacts and human remains they discovered. As technological breakthroughs increased the type of testing methods available and the number of archaeological sites being discovered grew, demand developed for specially trained professionals who could test artifacts and human and animal remains under precise scientific conditions. Today, archaeology laboratory testing technicians play an important role in analyzing objects and remains found at archaeological sites.

THE JOB

Laboratory testing technicians do the following when an object is brought into the laboratory: 1) conduct an overall examination of the artifact and review the field notes that have been submitted by field technicians, archaeologists, or other professionals; 2) clean the object if it is not too fragile; 3) catalog and number the object; 4) classify the object (by type of artifact, material, weight, length, color, noticeable markings, etc.); 5) restore or conserve the object as necessary; 6) conduct tests on the object (these include radiocarbon dating, bone mineral analysis, and soil flotation, among others); 7) process the information and record their findings in written reports and electronic databases; and 8) safely store the object.

Some basic equipment used by laboratory testing technicians includes strainers and geological screens, brushes, plastic and glass vials, bonding agents such as cement, screwdrivers, tweezers, dental picks, eyedroppers, magnifying glasses, beakers, magnets, scales, calipers, and microscopes.

Regardless of the specific nature of the tests conducted by technicians, they must always keep detailed records of every step. Laboratory technicians often do a great deal of writing and must make charts, graphs, and other displays to illustrate results. They may be called on to interpret test results, to draw overall conclusions, and to make recommendations.

Laboratory testing technicians must be comfortable using computer software programs such as Microsoft Word, Access, and Excel and computer graphic programs. Some laboratories require their technicians to have basic proficiency in geographic information system software such as ArcGIS. They use these programs to keep collections organized, track work done on each artifact, and complete paperwork that must be submitted to government agencies. Some archaeology laboratories are even placing information about their collections online for researchers and the general public to view. Laboratory testing technicians may help prepare these online databases.

REQUIREMENTS

High School

If working as a laboratory testing technician sounds interesting to you, you can prepare for this work by taking at least two years of mathematics and a year each of chemistry and physics in high school. You should also consider taking shop classes to become accustomed to working with tools and to develop manual dexterity. Classes in English and writing will provide you with good experience doing research and writing reports. Take computer classes so that you become familiar with using this tool. If you know that you want to specialize in archaeology, take relevant courses such as earth science, biology, geology, and archaeology.

Postsecondary Training

An associate's degree is the minimum requirement for finding work as a laboratory testing technician in the field of archaeology. How-

A laboratory technician (*left*) and an archaeologist carry a fusion of brick and armor metal to the site laboratory after removing it from the Jamestown well in Jamestown, Virginia. The well is believed to date to 1615. (*Dave Bowman, AP Photo*/The Daily Press)

ever, many employers are now seeking applicants with bachelor's degrees. Degree paths for laboratory testing technicians vary. Some technicians earn associate's or bachelor's degrees in archaeology or anthropology, while others pursue degrees in applied science or science-related technology. Many college programs incorporate an internship with a local employer into their curriculum.

Certification or Licensing
There is no certification available for laboratory testing technicians who specialize in archaeology. Those who work with human remains may need to be licensed by the state in which they are employed.

Other Requirements
Laboratory technicians should be detail oriented and enjoy figuring out how things work. They should like problem solving and trouble-shooting. Laboratory technicians must have the patience to repeat a test many times, perhaps even on the same material. They must be able to follow directions carefully but also should be independent and motivated to work on their own until their assigned tasks are completed.

EXPLORING

Due to the precision and training required in the field, it is unlikely that as a high school student you will be able to find a part-time or summer job as a laboratory testing technician. However, you can explore the career by contacting local technical colleges and arranging to speak with a professor in the school's technician program. Ask about the required classes, the opportunities available in your area, and any other questions you have. Through this connection you may also be able to contact a graduate of the program and arrange for an information interview with him or her. Although you probably won't be able to get work as a laboratory testing technician at this point, some contract archaeology companies and government agencies do offer summer jobs to high school students to work in their offices or mail rooms. While these jobs do not offer hands-on technical experience, they do allow you to experience the work environment.

EMPLOYERS

Laboratory testing technicians are employed by universities and community colleges, laboratories, contract archaeology companies, museums, and government agencies at all levels.

Laboratory technicians who work outside of the field of archaeology are employed in almost every type of manufacturing industry that employs chemists or chemical engineers. They are needed wherever testing is carried on, whether it is for developing new products or improving current manufacturing procedures or for quality control purposes. They also can find positions in research institutions and in government laboratories, such as those run by the federal Departments of Health, Agriculture, and Commerce.

STARTING OUT

Technical schools often help place graduating technicians. Many laboratories contact these schools directly looking for student employees or interns. Students can also contact local archaeology laboratories and contract archaeology firms to inquire about job openings in their area. Technicians often begin as trainees who are supervised by more experienced workers. As they gain experience, technicians take on more responsibilities and are allowed to work more independently.

Many archaeology professional associations and organizations offer job listings at their Web sites. Other Web sites that provide job listings include Earthworks-jobs.com (http://www.earthworks-jobs.com), Simply Hired (http://www.simplyhired.com), eCulturalResources (http://www.eculturalresources.com/jobs.php), and ArchaeologyFieldwork.com (http://www.archaeologyfieldwork.com).

ADVANCEMENT

Skilled laboratory technicians may be promoted to manager or supervisor of a division in their company. Experienced technicians may start their own testing laboratories or return to school to become archaeologists, chemists, or geologists.

EARNINGS

Earnings for laboratory testing technicians vary based on the type of work they do, their education and experience, and even the size of the laboratory and its location. The U.S. Department of Labor reports the following median annual earnings for science technicians (a category that includes laboratory testing technicians) in 2009 by specialty: biological technicians, $38,700; chemical technicians, $42,070; forensic science technicians, $51,480; and geological and petroleum technicians, $53,240. Salaries for science technicians ranged from less than $25,540 to $96,110 or more.

Salaries increase as technicians gain experience and as they take on supervisory responsibility. Most companies and government agencies that employ laboratory testing technicians offer medical benefits, sick leave, and vacation time. However, these benefits will depend on the individual employer.

WORK ENVIRONMENT

Laboratory testing technicians typically work a 40-hour week. During especially busy times or in special circumstances, they may be required to work overtime. Most technicians work in clean, well-lighted laboratories where attention is paid to neatness and organization. Some laboratory testing technicians have their own offices, while others work in large single-room laboratories.

Some technicians may be required to go outside their laboratories to test artifacts or remains at archaeological sites, which can be hot, cold, wet, muddy, and uncomfortable.

OUTLOOK

Overall, employment for science technicians (a category that includes laboratory testing technicians) is expected to grow about as fast as the average for all occupations through 2018, according to the U.S. Department of Labor. As new testing methods emerge for artifacts and human and animal remains, demand should continue for laboratory testing technicians.

Employment possibilities at testing laboratories will be affected by advances in technology. New testing procedures that are developed will lead to an increase in the testing that is done. However, increased automation will mean each technician can complete more work.

Technicians in any specialty who have strong educational backgrounds, keep up with developing technologies, and demonstrate knowledge of testing equipment will have the best employment opportunities.

FOR MORE INFORMATION

For information on careers in biological testing, contact
American Institute of Biological Sciences
1444 I Street, NW, Suite 200
Washington, DC 20005-6535
Tel: 202-628-1500
http://www.aibs.org

The ACS provides information on careers and new developments in the field.
American Chemical Society (ACS)
1155 16th Street, NW
Washington, DC 20036-4801
Tel: 800-227-5558
E-mail: help@acs.org
http://www.acs.org

To read Careers in Botany *and* Botany for the Next Millennium, *visit the society's Web site.*
Botanical Society of America
PO Box 299
St. Louis, MO 63166-0299
Tel: 314-577-9566
E-mail: bsa-manager@botany.org
http://www.botany.org

For career information, contact
Geological Society of America
Archaeological Geology Division

PO Box 9140
Boulder, CO 80301-9140
Tel: 888-443-4472
E-mail: gsaservice@geosociety.org
http://www.geosociety.org
http://rock.geosociety.org/arch

For information on archaeology careers, contact
Society for American Archaeology
900 Second Street, NE, Suite 12
Washington, DC 20002-3560
Tel: 202-789-8200
E-mail: headquarters@saa.org
http://www.saa.org

The SAS is an association for "those interested in advancing our knowledge of the past through a wide range of techniques deriving from the fields of physics, chemistry, and the natural sciences." Visit its Web site for more information.
Society for Archaeological Sciences (SAS)
http://www.socarchsci.org

For information on archaeology careers, contact
Society for Historical Archaeology
9707 Key West Avenue, Suite 100
Rockville, MD 20850-3992
Tel: 301-990-2454
E-mail: hq@sha.org
http://www.sha.org
http://www.sha.org/EHA/splash.cfm

Museum Curators

OVERVIEW

Museum curators care for objects in a museum's collection. In an archaeology museum, these items might consist of pottery, metalwork, textiles, weapons, tools, artwork, and any other object that has been created or altered by humans. Their primary curatorial activities are maintenance, preservation, archiving, cataloguing, study, and display of collection components. Curators must fundraise to support staff in the physical care and study of collections. They also add to or alter a museum's collection by trading or loaning objects with other museums or purchasing new pieces. They educate others through scholarly articles and public programs that showcase the items. There are approximately 11,700 curators employed in all types of museums and related facilities in the United States.

HISTORY

People have collected and displayed art, cultural items, artifacts, and other objects in museums or private residences for thousands of years, but it was not until the 1600s in Europe that the first public museums opened.

The forerunners of museums in colonial America were "cabinets of curiosities," or collections of unrelated objects that caught the imagination of collectors. These cabinets, which saw greatest growth in the early to mid-1700s, were often attached to a library society or college. They were not open to the general public, but available by subscription to members of the upper classes.

The Philadelphia Museum, a natural history museum that opened in 1786, is considered the prototype for the public museums that we

A curator of the Near East collection at The University of Pennsylvania Museum of Archaeology and Anthropology in Philadelphia sits near replicas of ancient items thought to have been stolen from the National Museum of Antiquities in Baghdad, Iraq. Archaeologists from the museum helped catalog the losses at Iraq's plundered national museum, relying in part on the university's own collection of artifacts from the region. *(Jacqueline Larma, AP Photo)*

are familiar with today. It was opened by Charles Willson Peale. Trained as a painter and saddlemaker, Peale developed the first formula for permanent preservation of species. He mounted the specimens in natural attitudes, posed them against habitat backgrounds he had painted, and labeled them according to the Linnean system of classification into genera and species.

The great period of museum building in the United States spanned more than a century, extending from the Age of Enlightenment through the Industrial Age. There was an impetus to build museums as a result of the many expeditions of exploration across the United States and in the waters of the Pacific, from which many exotic specimens and cultural artifacts from indigenous peoples were returned to cities on the eastern seaboard. In fact, the problem of warehousing so many articles was a crucial factor in the establishment of a national museum. The first national museum, the Smithsonian Institution, was established in 1846. The large variety of specimens, particularly those returned by explorers in the Pacific in the years 1838–42, led to the separation of art and natural history into distinct museums within the Smithsonian. (Today, there is even a Smithsonian museum that focuses solely on Native American history.) Other museums founded in the golden age of museum building included the Boston Museum of Fine Arts, the American Museum of Natural History in New York, the Art Institute of Chicago, and the Field Columbian Museum, later renamed the Field Museum of Natural History, also in Chicago.

In the early days of "cabinets of curiosities," the owners of these collections served as curators, but they usually had little training in the preservation, cataloguing, and proper display of these items. During the great period of museum building in the United States, the career of curator emerged as a professional position that required postsecondary training.

Today, curators (along with directors) are the professions that are most closely identified with the image and purposes of a museum. Highly trained curators help museums display their collections in a professional and attractive manner.

THE JOB

A curator's chief responsibilities include study and preservation of the museum's collections. Depending on the museum's size, resources, and deployment of staff, those responsibilities may be expressed in several different directions. In museums with a large curatorial staff, senior curators may function primarily as administrators, overseeing departmental budgets and hiring new curators. In a different employment environment, curators may focus closely on the study and shape of the collections, exchanging materials with other museums or acquiring new specimens and artifacts to create a representative study collection of importance to scholarly work. In a third type of environment, curators may be primarily educators who describe and present collections to the visiting public. At any time, museum administrators may ask curators to redirect efforts toward a different goal of priority to the museum. Thus, a curator develops or brings to the position substantial knowledge of the materials in the collection (for example, Anasazi pottery, Inca and Chimu metalwork, ancient Egyptian funerary objects, or textiles from the Ming Dynasty in China) and that knowledge is used by the museum for a changing mix of purposes over time.

Curators may also spend time in the field or as visiting scholars at other museums as a means of continuing research related to the home institution's collections. Fieldwork is usually supported by grants from external sources. As specialists in their disciplines, curators may teach classes in local schools and universities, sometimes serving as academic advisers to doctoral degree candidates whose research is based on museum holdings. Almost all curators supervise a staff ranging from volunteers, interns, and students to research associates, collections managers, technicians, junior curators, and secretarial staff. Some sort of written work, whether it is labeling exhibits, preparing brochures for museum visitors, or publishing in scholarly journals, is typically part of the position.

Museums on the Web

The Bodrum Museum of Underwater Archaeology
http://www.bodrum-museum.com

The Burke Museum of Natural History and Culture (University of Washington)
https://www.washington.edu/burkemuseum

Dickson Mounds Museum
http://www.museum.state.il.us/ismsites/dickson

El Paso Museum of Archaeology
http://www.elpasotexas.gov/arch_museum

Field Museum of Natural History
http://www.fieldmuseum.org

Haffenreffer Museum of Anthropology (Brown University)
http://www.brown.edu/Facilities/Haffenreffer

Kelsey Museum of Archaeology (University of Michigan)
http://www.lsa.umich.edu/kelsey

Logan Museum of Anthropology (Beloit College)
http://www.beloit.edu/logan

Maxwell Museum of Anthropology (University of New Mexico)
http://www.unm.edu/~maxwell

Mitchell Museum of the American Indian
http://www.mitchellmuseum.org

In related positions, *collections managers* and *curatorial assistants* perform many of the same functions as curators, with more emphasis on study and cataloguing of the collections and less involvement with administration and staff supervision. The educational requirements for these positions may be the same as for a curatorial position. A curatorial candidate may accept a position as collections manager while awaiting a vacancy on the curatorial staff, since the opportunity to study, publish research, and conduct fieldwork is usually equally available in both positions. In art, historical, archaeology, and anthro-

Museum of Art and Archaeology (University of Missouri)
http://maa.missouri.edu

Museum of Ontario Archaeology
http://www.uwo.ca/museum

Peabody Museum of Archaeology & Ethnology (Harvard University)
http://www.peabody.harvard.edu

San Diego Archaeological Center
http://www.sandiegoarchaeology.org

Simon Fraser University Museum of Archaeology and Ethnology
http://www.sfu.ca/archaeology/museum

Smithsonian Institution National Museum of Natural History
http://www.mnh.si.edu

Smithsonian Institution National Museum of the American Indian
http://www.nmai.si.edu

University of Denver Museum of Anthropology
http://www.du.edu/ahss/schools/anthropology/museum

University of Pennsylvania Museum of Archaeology and Anthropology
http://www.penn.museum

Western Science Center
http://westerncentermuseum.org

pological museums, registrars and archivists may act as collections managers by cataloguing and preserving documents and objects and making information on these items available for scholarly use.

Once hired, curators embark on what is essentially a lifelong program of continuing self-education in museum practices. Curators of large collections must remain current with preservation techniques, including climate control and pest control methods. The human working environment can affect collections in unpredictable ways.

An important development in collections management is computerized cataloguing of holdings for registry in national electronic databases. A number of larger museums and universities are working together to standardize data entry fields for these electronic registries, after which data on every item in a collection must be entered by hand and cross-checked for accuracy. Concurrently, there is a trend toward publishing through nonprint media, such as academic networks administered by the National Sciences Foundation. Continuing self-education in electronic technologies and participation in national conferences addressing these issues will be expected of curators throughout the upcoming decade and beyond, for electronic storage and retrieval systems have radically changed the face of collections management.

REQUIREMENTS

High School

Museum curators need diverse educational backgrounds to perform well in their jobs. At the high school level, you should take courses in English, literature, creative writing, history, art, the sciences, speech, business, and foreign language. These courses will give you the general background knowledge needed to understand both the educational and administrative functions of museums. Math and computer skills are also essential. If you want to work as a curator in a history-, archaeology-, or anthropology-related museum, you should take courses in science, anthropology, archaeology, history, and other related fields.

Postsecondary Training

While some small museums may hire curators with a bachelor's degree, most museums require that curatorial candidates have a master's degree. Some colleges and universities offer undergraduate degrees in museology, or the study of museums. Most museums require their chief curators to hold doctoral degrees. Curators usually work in museums that specialize in art, history (including anthropology and archaeology), or science. These individuals often have degrees in fields related to the museum's specialty. For example, a curator who is employed by an archaeology museum will have one or more degrees in archaeology, anthropology, or history. The most attractive job candidates have two graduate degrees: one in museology and one in archaeology, anthropology, or a related discipline. All curators must have a good working knowledge of the objects and cultures represented in their collections.

Other Requirements

Excellent written and oral communication skills are essential. Curators must have strong research skills and be able to help raise funds for projects when necessary. They must be able to meet deadlines, write scholarly articles, and give presentations while managing their traditional museum duties. Museum curators should be well organized and flexible.

Occasionally museums have specific requirements, such as foreign language fluency for an art or anthropology museum or practical computer skills for a science or natural history museum. These skills are ordinarily acquired as part of the background study within the student's area of concentration and do not pose special problems.

EXPLORING

Read books about careers in museums. Visit Web sites that provide more information on archaeology. Ask your counselor to arrange an information interview with a curator or a tour of a museum near you.

Archaeology and history museums offer public programs for people of all ages. Field trips or tours introduce students to activities conducted by local museums. You may consider participating in an archaeological dig. College-age students may work at museums as volunteers or perhaps as interns for course credit. Depending on the museum's needs, volunteers and interns may be placed anywhere in the museum, including administration, archives, and other areas where a student may observe staff functions firsthand. The American Association of Museums offers a list of member museums, as well as general information about museum careers, at its Web site, http://www.aam-us.org.

EMPLOYERS

Approximately 11,700 curators are employed in all types of museums and related facilities in the United States. Museums as well as historical societies and state and federal agencies with public archives and libraries hire curators. These institutions are located throughout the world, in both small and large cities, and are responsible for providing public access to their collections. Museums and similar institutions employ curators to fulfill their educational goals through continued research, care of collections, and public programs.

STARTING OUT

Museology, or the study of museums, is offered as an undergraduate major by some colleges in the United States, but most museum workers at all levels enter museum work because they possess specific skills and a body of knowledge useful to a particular museum. For a curator, this translates into content knowledge, managerial and administrative skills, fund-raising ability, leadership ability, and excellent communication skills for effective interaction with the media and the board of trustees. While the role of a curator is focused primarily on collections, the position requires a great degree of knowledge across the board regarding the museum's mission statement, acquisitions, and community involvement.

A position as curator usually is not anticipated and prepared for in advance, but becomes available as an employment option following a long period of training in a discipline. College and advanced degree students who have identified a curatorial position as a career goal may be able to apply for curatorial internships of varying terms, usually a year or less. Interns typically work on a project identified by the museum, which may involve only one task or several different tasks. Additionally, museums thrive on a large base of volunteer labor, and this method of gaining museum experience should not be overlooked. Curators may ask volunteers to assist in a variety of tasks, ranging from clerical duties to conservation and computerized cataloguing. When funds are available, volunteer work may be converted to hourly paid work.

ADVANCEMENT

Museum curatorial positions follow the assistant, associate, and full (or senior) track of academic employment, with advancement depending on research and publishing, education, and service to the institution. A curator with a taste for and skill in administration may serve as departmental chair or may seek a higher administrative post such as museum director.

In the course of their museum duties, curators may act as advisers to or principals in external nonprofit endeavors, such as providing technical assistance and labor to aid a developing country in the study of its archaeological past. Many teach in local schools or universities. Curators who leave museum work may devote themselves full time to these or similar pursuits, although a university professorship as a second choice is difficult to achieve, for curators and professors are essentially competing for the same market position and have similar credentials. Occasionally, curators find fieldwork so compelling that they leave not only the museum, but also all formal employment, relying on grants and personal contributions from supporters to support their work. To maintain an independent life as a researcher without formal affiliation requires a high profile in the discipline, continuing demonstration of productivity in the form of new research and publications, and some skill in self-promotion.

EARNINGS

The salaries of museum curators cover a broad range, reflecting the diversity, size, and budget of U.S. museums, along with the curator's academic and professional achievements. In general, museum workers' salaries are low compared to salaries for similar positions in the business world or in academia. This is due in part to the large number of people competing for the relatively small number of positions available. Curators directing an ongoing program of conservation and acquisitions in a large, national or international urban museum command the highest salaries and may earn average annual salaries of more than $90,205 a year.

According to the U.S. Department of Labor (DOL), the median annual earnings of curators were $47,930 in 2009. Salaries ranged from less than $27,000 to more than $83,900. The DOL reports that museum curators earned the following mean annual salaries by employer in 2009: colleges, universities, and professional schools, $58,020; local government, $52,860; and museums, historical sites, and similar institutions, $48,640.

Fringe benefits, including paid vacations and sick leave, medical and dental insurance, and retirement plans are usually available, but vary by each employing institution's policies.

WORK ENVIRONMENT

Curators typically have an office in a private area of the museum, but may have to share office space. Employment conditions and benefits are more like those of industry than academia, although the employment contract may stipulate that the curator is free to pursue a personal schedule of fieldwork for several weeks during the year.

A curatorial post is typically a 9-to-5 job, but that does not take into account the long hours of study necessary to sustain scholarly

research, weekend time spent on public programs, or evening meetings with donors, trustees, and museum affiliates. The actual hours
spent on curatorial-related activities may be double those of the
employment contract. Curators must enjoy their work, be interested
in museum operations and a museum's profile in the community, and
willingly put in the necessary time. Curatorial positions are won by
highly educated, versatile people, who in turn accept long hours and
relatively (in comparison to other industries) low pay in exchange for
doing work they love.

OUTLOOK

Employment for museum curators is expected to increase much
faster than the average for all occupations through 2018, according
to the *Occupational Outlook Handbook*. Despite this prediction,
there are few openings for curators at archaeology museums and
competition for them is high. New graduates may have to start as
interns, volunteers, assistants, or research associates before finding
a full-time curator position. Turnover is very low in museum work,
so museum workers may have to stay in a lower-level position for
some years before advancing to a curator position.

Curators must be able to develop revenue-generating public programs based on the study collections and integrate themselves firmly
into programs of joint research with area institutions (other museums or universities) or national institutions, ideally programs of
some duration and supported by external funding. Museums are
affected by economic conditions and the availability of grants and
other charitable funding.

FOR MORE INFORMATION

*For information on careers, education and training, and intern-
ships, contact*
   American Association of Museums
   1575 Eye Street, NW, Suite 400
   Washington, DC 20005-1113
   Tel: 202-289-1818
   http://www.aam-us.org

Private Sector Archaeologists

OVERVIEW

Archaeologists study the origin and evolution of humans. They study the physical evidence of human culture, examining such items as tools, burial sites, structures, religious items, ceramics, and textiles. Archaeologists employed in the private sector work for a variety of employers such as cultural resources management (CRM) firms, private museums and cultural centers, and private colleges and universities.

HISTORY

It wasn't until the 19th century that archaeology became an established discipline. The excavation of archaeological sites has provided information about cultures that lived during the Ice Age, the development of agriculture, the civilizations of the ancient Egyptians and the Anasazi, and other prehistoric and historical cultures and events.

The majority of early archaeological research and fieldwork in the United States was funded by government agencies at the local, state, and federal levels, as well as government-funded museums, cultural centers, and colleges and universities.

In the late 1960s, private sector archaeology became more prevalent as a result of the passage of three laws: the National Historic Preservation Act of 1966, the Department of Transportation Act of 1966, and the National Environmental Policy Act of 1969. These laws required U.S. federal government agencies to consider the archaeological,

QUICK FACTS

School Subjects
Art
Foreign language
History

Personal Skills
Communication/ideas
Leadership/management
Technical/scientific

Work Environment
Indoors and outdoors
Primarily multiple locations

Minimum Education Level
Bachelor's degree

Salary Range
$31,530 to $65,130 to $119,070+

Certification or Licensing
Voluntary

Outlook
Much faster than the average

DOT
054, 090

GOE
02.04.01, 12.03.02

NOC
4121, 4169

O*NET-SOC
19-3091.00, 19-3091.02, 25-1061.00

historical, and cultural impact of any construction or land use projects that were undertaken on federal lands, that were funded by the federal government but on private lands, or those that required a permit from the federal government (such as areas where cell towers are constructed). Soon thereafter, tribal, state, and local governments also began developing CRM programs. These developments created a strong demand for companies to conduct CRM surveys and excavations. Today, CRM archaeology comprises at least 90 percent of all field archaeology that is conducted in the United States, according to *Archaeology Essentials: Theories, Methods, and Practice,* by Colin Renfrew and Paul Bahn.

In addition to employment in cultural resources management, private sector archaeologists also work in academic or research archaeology at museums, cultural centers, and colleges and universities.

THE JOB

Archaeologists in both the private and public sectors apply specialized techniques to construct a record of past cultures by studying, classifying, and interpreting artifacts such as pottery, clothing, tools, weapons, and ornaments, to determine cultural identity. They obtain these artifacts through excavation of sites including buildings and cities, and they establish the chronological sequence of the development of each culture from simpler to more advanced levels. *Prehistoric archaeologists* study cultures that existed prior to the period of recorded history, while *historical archaeologists* study more recent societies. The historic period spans several thousand years in some parts of the world and sometimes only a few hundred years in others. *Classical archaeologists* concentrate on ancient Mediterranean and Middle Eastern cultures. Through the study of the history of specific groups of peoples whose societies may be extinct, archaeologists are able to reconstruct their cultures, including the pattern of daily life. As faculty members of colleges and universities, archaeologists lecture on the subject, work with research assistants, and publish books and articles.

Before the 1960s, archaeological excavations were large in scale. Archaeologists preferred to clear as much land as possible, hoping to uncover a large volume of artifacts. But today's archaeologists understand that much can be lost in an excavation, and they limit their studies to smaller areas. With radar, sensors, and other technologies, archaeologists can discover a great deal about a site before any actual digging is undertaken. They also deliberately leave some areas untouched so that future archaeologists can apply new technologies and excavation techniques to research at the site.

Archaeologists often must travel extensively to perform fieldwork on the site where a culture once flourished. Site work is often slow and laborious. It may take years to uncover artifacts from an archaeological dig that produce valuable information. Another important aspect of archaeology is the cleaning, restoration, and preservation of artifacts. This work sometimes takes place on the site of discovery to minimize deterioration of textiles and mummified remains. Careful recording of the exact location and condition of artifacts is essential for further study. This type of work is also conducted in laboratories.

Private sector archaeologists are employed by CRM firms, engineering and environmental companies that provide CRM services, laboratories, companies that specialize in archaeological investigation and excavation, private museums and cultural centers, and private colleges and universities. The following paragraphs provide an overview of job responsibilities and titles for archaeologists who work for various private sector employers.

Cultural resources management firms/engineering and environmental companies that provide CRM services. Cultural resources can be defined as important archaeological sites and objects, historical structures, cultural landscapes, and ethnographic resources. Archaeologists employed at CRM firms are hired to conduct surveys of construction and land-use sites (such as buildings, roads, bridges, highways, and dams) to determine if they contain cultural resources that must be protected or preserved under local, state, nation, or tribal CRM laws and regulations. Archaeologists first review blueprints and construction plans to determine if the area contains any known archaeological sites. Then they travel to the site to conduct a visual survey and conduct shovel tests, very small excavations that help determine if artifacts, structures, and/or remains are present. If they locate such materials, archaeologists conduct a more thorough excavation. These tests are done to determine if significant collections of artifacts (called cultural deposits) are present. If found, these materials are then sent to a laboratory for analysis. If culturally significant sites are discovered, the construction plan is revised to avoid the areas, or the sites are excavated before construction begins. CRM archaeologists then clean, sort, identify, label, conserve, and catalog the items. They also write reports that summarize their work for government agencies.

Laboratories. Archaeologists employed by laboratories study artifacts that range from charcoal collected from prehistoric fire pits, to arrowheads and bullets from battlefields, to ceramics and textiles, to plant residues and human remains recovered from ancient shipwrecks. They also record their findings in written reports and electronic databases. Some archaeologists employed by laboratories also conduct fieldwork.

Companies that specialize in archaeological investigation and excavation. Archaeologists employed by these types of companies might perform contract archaeology for cultural resources management firms or conduct archaeological fieldwork for museums, cultural centers, or colleges and universities.

Private museums and cultural centers. Archaeologists employed in these settings work on organization-sponsored archaeological digs and conduct research in museum laboratories and office settings. They also serve as *museum educators* and, with additional education, *museum directors* and *curators*. The museum director is responsible for the daily operations of the museum, for long-term planning, policies, any research conducted within the museum, and for the museum's fiscal health. Museum curators care for objects in a museum's collection. The primary curatorial activities are maintenance, preservation, archiving, cataloguing, study, and display of collection components. They also conduct fund-raising to help pay for the operation of their institutions.

Private colleges and universities. Archaeologists employed in academic settings work as *teachers*. They teach classes, lead fieldwork, and otherwise conduct research in their specialty, such as archaeobotany, ethnoarchaeology, archaeogeology, or underwater archaeology.

REQUIREMENTS

High School
In high school, take a college preparatory track that includes classes in science, mathematics, and history. English and speech classes will help you write reports and communicate effectively with coworkers. These courses will be especially useful to archaeologists who plan to work as educators. Computer science will teach you how to work with databases, use software programs, and prepare presentations. Taking one or more foreign languages is also recommended.

Postsecondary Training
The minimum educational requirements for private sector archaeologists is a bachelor's degree in archaeology, anthropology, history, historic preservation, or a related field. A degree at this level will allow you to work in entry-level positions in laboratories or in the field. You will need a minimum of a master's degree to qualify for most positions. A master's or doctorate is required for work as a college educator. Museum directors and curators must have at least

a bachelor's degree for employment in some smaller museums, but a master's degree is typically required to work for large museums. Most museums require their directors and chief curators to hold doctoral degrees. Some colleges and universities offer undergraduate degrees in museology, or the study of museums.

Archaeology departments are typically part of anthropology departments; few separate archaeology departments exist in U.S. colleges and universities. In addition to classwork, most students participate in internships or field schools, where they learn how to conduct archaeological fieldwork and laboratory research.

Certification or Licensing

The Register of Professional Archaeologists offers voluntary registration to archaeologists who agree to "abide by an explicit code of conduct and standards of research performance; who hold a graduate degree in archaeology, anthropology, art history, classics, history, or another germane discipline; and who have substantial practical experience."

Other Requirements

Key traits for archaeologists include excellent communication skills, an analytical personality, the ability to solve problems, strong organizational talents, the ability to get along well with others and work as a member of a team, excellent time management skills (especially for those who work as CRM archaeologists), and a willingness to continue to learn throughout their careers.

EXPLORING

An excellent way to learn more about archaeology is to read books and magazines about the field. Here are a few book suggestions: *Archaeology For Dummies,* by Nancy Marie White (Hoboken, N.J.: For Dummies, 2008); *Practicing Archaeology: An Introduction to Cultural Resources Archaeology,* 2d ed., by Thomas W. Neumann (Lanham, Md.: AltaMira Press, 2009); and *Archaeology,* 5th ed., by Robert L. Kelly and David Hurst Thomas (Florence, Ky.: Wadsworth Publishing, 2009). Interesting periodicals to check out include *American Archaeology* (http://www.americanarchaeology.com/aa magazine.html) and *Archaeology* (http://www.archaeology.org).

Another way to learn more about archaeology is to participate in an archaeological dig during your summer vacation. Digs are typically sponsored by government agencies, colleges and universities, and private sector organizations. Visit the Web sites of the following organizations for more information on participating in an archaeological field expedition: Crow Canyon Archaeological Center (http://www.crowcanyon.org), Center for American Archaeology (http://www.caa-archeology.org), and the Shumla School (http://www.shumla.org).

You can also ask a teacher or counselor to arrange an information interview with an archaeologist. This is a great way to learn more about the field and possible career paths.

EMPLOYERS

Private sector archaeologists are employed by cultural resources management firms, engineering and environmental companies that provide CRM services, laboratories, companies that specialize in archaeological investigation and excavation, private museums and cultural centers, and private colleges and universities.

STARTING OUT

College career services offices and professors can provide job listings for work in the private sector. Many students learn about job opportunities and make valuable networking contacts while participating in internships and field schools. Direct application to employers is also recommended; many employers list job openings at their Web sites.

Professional associations and organizations that offer job listings at their Web sites include the Archaeological Institute of America (http://www.archaeological.org), the Society for Historical Archaeology (http://www.sha.org/students_jobs), and the Society for American Archaeology (http://www.saa.org).

There are also many archaeology-oriented employment sites that provide job listings, including Earthworks-jobs.com (http://www.earthworks-jobs.com), eCulturalResources (http://www.ecultural resources.com/jobs.php), and ArchaeologyFieldwork.com (http://www.archaeologyfieldwork.com).

ADVANCEMENT

Archaeologists advance by receiving higher pay, working on larger or more prestigious projects, or being asked to supervise workers or manage entire projects. They also write books and articles about their work and appear as experts on radio and television shows and in film documentaries. Curators and directors advance by earning higher pay or finding employment at larger, better-known museums. College teachers advance from instructor to assistant professor, to associate professor, to full professor. Others become department heads or university presidents.

EARNINGS

The U.S. Department of Labor (DOL) reports that salaries for archaeologists employed in all settings ranged from less than $31,530 to $87,890 or more in 2009. Mean annual earnings for private sector and government archaeologists employed at museums, historical sites, and similar institutions were $55,150. The DOL reports the following mean annual salaries for private sector archaeologists by type of employer: architectural, engineering, and related services, $65,130; scientific research and development services, $51,620; and management, scientific, and technical consulting services, $49,470.

Many archaeologists work in academia. According to the DOL, college and university archaeology professors earned between $41,270 and $119,070 in 2009, depending on the type of institution. Median annual earnings were $69,520.

Benefits for full-time workers include paid vacation, health, disability, life insurance, and retirement or pension plans.

WORK ENVIRONMENT

Work settings for private sector archaeologists vary greatly by type of employer. Some archaeologists work indoors in classrooms, laboratories, offices, and museums. Others spend most of their time in the field at archaeological digs and work in a variety of environments (grasslands, deserts, mountains, underwater, rainforests, tundra, caves, etc.) and weather conditions (although most archaeological digs shut down as soon as the ground freezes). Most private sector archaeologists work 40 hours a week, with overtime (especially for CRM archaeologists) required when a project is on deadline.

OUTLOOK

The U.S. Department of Labor predicts that employment for archaeologists will grow much faster than the average for all occupations through 2018. The employment outlook in the private sector varies by employer. Overall, the number of job applicants for university faculty positions will be greater than the number of openings available. Competition will be great even for those with doctorates who are seeking faculty positions, and many will find only temporary or non-tenured jobs. Only a small number of archaeologists are employed as museum educators, curators, and directors—making it difficult to land a job in these fields.

The employment outlook for archaeologists employed in cultural resources management is expected to be excellent. Among the factors contributing to this growth is increased environmental, historic, and cultural preservation legislation. There is a particular demand for people with the ability to write environmental impact statements. A growing number of archaeologists will be employed by construction companies to perform salvage archaeology, in which quick excavation of artifacts is conducted before construction destroys a site.

FOR MORE INFORMATION

The following organization offers valuable information about anthropological careers and student associations:

American Anthropological Association
Archeology Division
2200 Wilson Boulevard, Suite 600
Arlington, VA 22201-3357
Tel: 703-528-1902
http://www.aaanet.org/sections/ad

For information on careers, education and training, and internships, contact

American Association of Museums
1575 Eye Street, NW, Suite 400
Washington, DC 20005-1113
Tel: 202-289-1818
http://www.aam-us.org

To read about the issues affecting college professors, contact the following organizations:

American Association of University Professors
1133 19th Street, NW, Suite 200
Washington, DC 20036-3655
Tel: 202-737-5900
E-mail: aaup@aaup.org
http://www.aaup.org

American Federation of Teachers
555 New Jersey Avenue, NW
Washington, DC 20001-2029
Tel: 202-879-4400
http://www.aft.org

For industry information, contact
American Cultural Resources Association
5024-R Campbell Boulevard
Baltimore, MD 21236-5943
Tel: 410-933-3483
http://www.acra-crm.org

For an overview of the career of archaeologist written by an associate professor of anthropology, visit
Frequently Asked Questions About a Career in Archaeology in the U.S.
http://www.museum.state.il.us/ismdepts/anthro/dlcfaq.html

For information on professional registration, contact
Register of Professional Archaeologists
5024-R Campbell Boulevard
Baltimore, MD 21236-5943
Tel: 410-933-3486
E-mail: info@rpanet.org
http://www.rpanet.org

For information on archaeology careers and job listings, contact
Society for American Archaeology
900 Second Street, NE, Suite 12
Washington, DC 20002-3560
Tel: 202-789-8200
E-mail: headquarters@saa.org
http://www.saa.org

The SAS is an association for "those interested in advancing our knowledge of the past through a wide range of techniques deriving from the fields of physics, chemistry, and the natural sciences." Visit its Web site for more information.
Society for Archaeological Sciences (SAS)
http://www.socarchsci.org

For career information, contact
Society for Historical Archaeology
9707 Key West Avenue, Suite 100
Rockville, MD 20850-3992
Tel: 301-990-2454
E-mail: hq@sha.org
http://www.sha.org
http://www.sha.org/EHA/splash.cfm

──── INTERVIEW ────

Dr. Rebecca Schwendler, RPA, is the public lands advocate for the Mountains/Plains Office of the National Trust for Historic Preservation in Denver, Colorado. She also has worked as a cultural resources senior project manager for SWCA Environmental Consultants. Dr. Schwendler discussed her career with the editors of Careers in Focus: Archaeology.

Q. What made you want to enter this career?

A. I remember visiting the Museum of Natural History in New York City as a young kid and loving the dinosaur skeletons, so I think that planted the seed of my wanting to study old things—although not nearly that old! In high school I plastered my locker and my closet at home with pictures of Indiana Jones, leopard spot tissue paper, and images of khaki field clothes from early Banana Republic catalogues. I liked the romantic idea of having an exotic, adventurous life filled with travel, outdoor activities, and unique experiences.

Then, as a junior in high school in Atlanta, I took a Biblical archaeology class from a great teacher. The specific topic was less important to me than the idea of digging in the dirt in a foreign land and sharing stories with other laid-back, interesting people. During the last few days of the spring class, after the seniors had graduated, we watched *Raiders of the Lost Ark*. While I knew that wasn't real (or ethical) archaeology, it fueled my romantic notions of a career in archaeology. Then, during my senior year of high school, I interned at the (now) Michael C. Carlos Museum of Art and Archaeology at Emory University for my mandatory "career week." In working with the director, curator, collections manager, and others, I knew that archaeology—and maybe even museum work—was the career for me. I loved that the young director at the time was fluent in multiple languages and I wanted to have a career in which I, too, developed those skills. In college at Tufts University, I majored in sociocultural anthropology because I wanted what I felt was a broader academic background, rather than a specific focus on archaeology. I took a couple archaeology classes at Tufts and then spent my junior year abroad at the University of Edinburgh in Scotland. There I took a year-long Scottish archaeology class and participated in my first excavation—on the island of Cyprus, in the middle of a banana field, overlooking the Mediterranean. Academically and personally it was a life-changing trip and fueled my desire to have a career in archaeology. By the time I graduated from Tufts, I knew absolutely that I wanted a hands-on career in which I could dig in the dirt, travel to foreign places, meet people from around the world, and learn new things about the past.

Just before I graduated from college, I was lucky enough to get a job at a cultural resources management firm in Atlanta and that's where I really learned about practicing archaeology from two great people, in particular.

Q. Please describe a day in your life on the job. What are your typical work responsibilities? Can you describe your work environment?

A. I'll answer this question from two very different perspectives—one as a former senior project manager at an environmental consulting firm, and one as the current public lands advocate for the National Trust for Historic Preservation (National Trust).

As a senior project manager, I was responsible for virtually every aspect of several archaeological projects in the public sector (i.e., work that fulfilled Section 106 requirements for development projects involving federal funds and/or permits). My tasks included writing proposals and developing budgets for archaeological projects; researching and writing about the prehistory and history of specific areas; developing research questions and creating research designs that included the number of excavation units, shovel tests, auger holes, or other tests that we would use to investigate areas and answer research questions; interviewing and hiring prospective field technicians to assist me on projects; using a global positioning system or a "total station" (computerized transit) to map sites; overseeing fieldwork; surveying or excavating; interpreting sites; taking daily notes and photographing sites; interpreting features such as fire pits and structures; analyzing stone artifacts; arranging for specialists to date and analyze other kinds of artifacts; writing reports; overseeing the production of site maps; keeping project budgets in line; communicating with clients and regulatory agencies about projects; and ensuring that artifacts and paperwork were curated after projects were completed. On a few projects, I also created educational materials such as handouts, posters, and small exhibits. I managed several projects at the same time, each of which was at a different stage, so on days when I was in the office, I often spent time on one or more of the above tasks for multiple projects. That required being very organized and being comfortable jumping back and forth between different projects. On days that I was in the field, I could focus on field-based activities for one specific project, although I sometimes had to call the office or clients from the field to talk about other projects I was managing. My days were sometimes hectic but always interesting because I juggled so many different responsibilities. The office environment ranged from laid-back to hectic, depending on how many crews were going into or coming back from the field. The company employs archaeologists, biologists, geographers, editors, and others so it was great to share information with people who were really interested in their fields and from whom I could learn about different topics. The work environment in the field also ranged from relaxed to hectic. While we usually had to work hard to meet project deadlines, we also generally really enjoyed being outside and often had fun chatting with one another in the evenings over dinner.

As a public lands advocate, my archaeological duties are very different. While I sometimes visit archaeological sites and talk to federal, state, and private archaeologists, I no longer manage field projects, survey or excavate sites, or analyze artifacts. Instead, I have more of an advisory, educational, and information-gathering role, as I provide an archaeological perspective on preservation issues and solutions. For example, I help to write comment letters about specific government projects that threaten cultural resources on federal public lands, and I help to prepare informative documents that argue for protecting specific locations and resources. As a grassroots advocate, I also collect information about preservation issues from archaeologists, Native American tribes, community members, and other concerned parties. In turn, I impart information to various individuals and organizations about federal protections for prehistoric, historic, and Native resources. My work environment is fairly calm because many (although not all) of the projects on which I work are ongoing and do not have immediate deadlines. Occasionally things get hectic if comment letters and information sheets are due around the same time. However, I spend much of my time reading up on current issues and projects on federal public lands; devising preservation strategies with other members of the National Trust's public lands team (based largely in Denver, Washington, D.C., and San Francisco); and communicating with partner preservation and environmental organizations to address specific federal projects. In addition, I have been helping to create a landing page about Native American Heritage in Preservation on the National Trust's Web site (http://www.preservationnation.org). Because my position is a new one, and because most people in my office do not work on public lands issues, I am defining my responsibilities as time goes on.

Q. What are the most important personal and professional qualities for people in your career?

A. Again, I'll answer this as both a practicing archaeologist and a public lands advocate because some of the qualities are different. I think the most important personal and professional qualities for archaeologists are patience, persistence, adaptability, inquisitiveness, knowledge of a great variety of subjects, and attention to detail. Important qualities for a public lands advocate, on the other hand, are persistence, passion for cultural resources and preservation, creativity, and knowledge of federal regulations. Archaeologists, whether in academia or the public sector, are judged on their ability to defend their ideas and positions based on facts and research. A public lands advocate would probably be judged more on his or her ability to make a good case for preservation, by evoking people's personal, emotional, and spiritual connections to specific places, as well as by citing laws that protect cultural resources.

Q. What are some of the pros and cons of your job?

A. As a practicing archaeologist, I loved traveling, working outside, learning about new places, getting to know new people, eating new foods, seeing unusual and amazing things, and having new and diverse experiences. Applying my archaeological skills and Ph.D. experience directly to my work and learning from practitioners in other fields was very satisfying. However, cons to being a practicing archaeologist were being away from home (and my significant other, animals, and friends) for extended or frequent periods of time, getting to know people and then never seeing them again, having to keep track of every minute of my time for billing purposes, having to meet many tight deadlines, and sometimes working very long hours in unpleasant weather. Another con was creating reports and doing work that usually "benefited" only a very small number of people.

The big pro of being a public lands advocate is potentially making a huge difference for literally thousands of cultural resources (e.g., archaeological sites, historic sites, and Native American sacred places) and for millions of people who will benefit from the resources' preservation. Another pro is traveling to new places and meeting new people, yet not being away from home for too long or working in the cold, heat, and poison ivy. Additional pros include sharing my passion for cultural resources with other people, learning preservation advocacy skills, and having the time to devote to promoting historic preservation in my own community. However, the cons of being a public lands advocate are not getting to directly use my archaeological skills, not having fellow public lands advocates with whom I can commiserate, and having to figure out how to effectively integrate archaeological voices into the preservation world.

Q. What is the employment outlook for your field?

A. While I have heard about some job losses in public sector archaeology, the employment outlook for the field generally remains good. The new [Obama] administration's emphasis on producing renewable energy on federal public lands and the continued building of new transmission lines, pipelines, roads, and other developments on public lands necessitate the employment of many archaeologists for Section 106 compliance work.

Through the generosity of a private donor, my current position is basically guaranteed for the next four years. I hope that the position will be renewed at the end of that term. However, I am currently the National Trust's only public lands advocate so the employment outlook for that specific position is extremely limited.

Q. What has been one (or more) of your most rewarding experiences in your career and why?

A. One of my most rewarding experiences as a public sector archaeologist was leading a long excavation project at a Pueblo III–IV site (ca. A.D. 1250 to 1350) in western New Mexico and then completing the project's large and complex report. The 14-week-long field stage allowed me to really become engaged in the place, the site, and the research questions. Furthermore, chatting with travelers using the adjacent road and with people from nearby small communities and the Pueblo of Zuni led me to better understand people's diverse knowledge and opinions about archaeology and prehistory. By spending months on the report, I also tested my skills in archaeological interpretation. Writing and creating a polished and informative final product was very satisfying and I loved designing informational posters to highlight what we learned from the project.

A completely different, yet equaling rewarding, experience was when I gave a guest presentation at an elementary school outside Denver. For three hours, the students were extremely engaged in the topic of archaeology, listening to my travel stories, picking up real and replica artifacts, asking questions about how archaeologists work, and learning diverse skills (e.g., math, reading comprehension, history) through archaeology. That morning, I truly felt that I was helping to inspire a future generation to better appreciate cultural resources and our collective human past.

As a public lands advocate, my most rewarding experience so far has been helping to get the National Trust actively involved in discussions about renewable energy production on federal public lands. Before a colleague of mine and I joined the National Trust just over a year ago, there was no national voice for cultural resources preservation on federal public lands. Now, however, environmental groups call on us to help write project-specific comment letters and to interact with Congress to find ways to preserve cultural resources while supporting renewable energy development. I'm rewarded by seeing the nation slowly become more aware of the great benefits of preserving all kinds of cultural resources.

Underwater Archaeologists

OVERVIEW

Underwater archaeology involves any archaeological work or investigation done under water or sediment. The field is sometimes broken into the following specialties: *nautical archaeology* (the study of shipbuilding and watercraft) and *maritime* or *marine archaeology* (the study of shipwrecks, ports, and seafaring cultures). Other underwater archaeologists specialize in studying artifacts from a particular era, such as the time of the Roman Empire. *Underwater archeologists* identify potential survey sites, conduct the excavation work, and bring items to the surface for further study and research.

HISTORY

Archaeologists have recovered artifacts from beneath water since the early days of professional archaeology, but these items were usually just brought to the surface for examination without extensive study while they were still underwater. These primitive techniques caused the loss of valuable information and the destruction of artifacts that might have been preserved if they were studied in their original surroundings.

According to the Institute of Nautical Archaeology, underwater archaeology as we understand it today began in 1960 when George Bass and a group of researchers established a camp on the coast of southwestern Turkey to excavate the wreck of a Phoenician merchant ship that had sunk around 1200 B.C. Bass and his team developed ground-breaking methods to record and scientifically study the underwater site instead of automatically bringing the artifacts to the surface. According to the institute, this was "the first ancient wreck excavated in its entirety on the seabed, and the first shipwreck excavation directed and published by a diving archaeologist." The techniques used by Bass and his team are still in use today.

Underwater archaeologists map out the position of objects in a shipwreck in the Florida Keys National Marine Sanctuary, near Key Largo, Florida. *(Wilfredo Lee, AP Photo)*

THE JOB

Underwater archaeologists, whether exploring an ancient shipwreck, a sunken port or city, a sacrificial well, or an entire submerged civilization, help find information and answer questions about different cultures. This information ranges from the types of ships built or construction used to build houses and other structures, to the types of goods that were traded or the everyday life of a civilization. Many of the sites discovered by underwater archeologists are well preserved due to their settings—lack of sunlight, extreme cold temperatures, or burial under protective sediment. Such settings keep artifacts well preserved and intact, giving archaeologists a wealth of information and insight regarding cultures or historical incidents that otherwise would have been lost.

When people think of underwater archaeology, large shipwrecks come to mind. The recovery of the *Titanic,* a large passenger liner that sank in 1912, is one such example. The discovery of this ill-fated ocean liner was a huge event. Underwater archeologists used global positioning satellite technology and side-scan sonar to locate the wreck and estimate its depth in the ocean. Archaeologists and underwater specialists then boarded submersibles complete with high-power lighting and underwater photography and videography equipment to study the wreck. Underwater archaeologists, during the course of many expeditions, were able to retrieve artifacts—even a portion of the ship's hull.

Underwater archeologists, especially when working in such conditions and depth, rely on a variety of techniques and tools to help them conduct research. They use a dredge or a suction hose (called an airlift) to remove sediment. (They may only use trowels to do very fine work.) Underwater archaeologists may lay out a grid of plastic pipes around the site to keep it organized and write on laminated tablets or plastic slates to record their findings. Water cranes or airlifts are used to help bring bulky or heavy items to the surface. Special water containers are used to help stabilize artifacts that have absorbed great amounts of saltwater or sediment. Latex molds of timber are also made to provide an accurate overview of how a ship was constructed. And because the watery depths can be very cold, heated salt water is pumped through hoses to warm the inside of underwater archaeologists' scuba suits.

Underwater archaeologists also need to have a detailed conservation plan ready once the articles are removed from the water. Artifacts can disintegrate quickly or shrivel if not conserved immediately after removal.

Underwater archeologists are also called upon to excavate cities or ports now submerged underwater due to gradually rising sea levels or natural disasters. One example is the excavation of the English colonial city of Port Royal in Jamaica, which was partially destroyed during a huge earthquake in 1692. Underwater archeologists spent many years investigating the site of the former city, and were surprised to learn that many of the city's buildings and structures were left intact. This was probably due to the fact that, during the earthquake, large tracts of the city sank directly down into layers of water-saturated sand in which the city had been built. During this type of excavation, underwater archeologists relied on tools such as remote-control roving submersibles to provide a better picture and location of the site. Water dredging techniques were also employed to quickly and safely remove centuries of layered sand and sediment. Due to the work of underwater archeologists, historians have a better idea of the architectural styles and construction methods of the time, including the types of building materials used. Excavation has also provided archaeologists with important information about the Port Royalist's diet, their cooking utensils, and other aspects of their daily lives. (Visit http://nautarch.tamu.edu/portroyal for detailed information on the archaeological investigation of Port Royal.)

Not all sites entail lost civilizations or shipwrecks. Many underwater archeological projects involve only a little water. Submerged remains of structures such as bridges, crannogs, or platforms are of interest to archeologists as are sinkholes, wells, springs, and shallow coastlines. There are even archaeologists who are licensed to dig in the muck along the Thames River in London. Such sites often hold information about past cultures, as well as information regarding plant and animal material, the surrounding landscape, effects of pollution, and climate during particular eras.

In addition to working in the field, many underwater archaeologists are employed as teachers at colleges and universities.

REQUIREMENTS
High School
Since underwater archaeologists need a college education to work in the field, you should pursue a college preparatory program in high school. Take English composition, literature, and speech to develop your writing, interpretation, and oral communication skills. History classes will teach you about past civilizations. Mathematics, science, and computer courses can help you develop the skills you'll need in analyzing information and statistics. This may help you later as you

conduct fieldwork in other countries. You should also learn how to swim and take scuba diving courses.

It is a good idea to take at least one foreign language. Recommended languages include French, Spanish, or German. Those who plan to pursue a career in Old World or Classical Archaeology should take Greek or Latin.

Postsecondary Training
You will need a doctorate to obtain the best positions in archaeology. The first step on your educational path is earning a bachelor's degree in archaeology, anthropology, history, or a related area. In addition to classes in these areas, you will also study such basic courses as psychology, sociology, history, geography, mathematics, logic, English composition, and literature, as well as modern and ancient languages. After you earn a bachelor's degree, you will need to pursue graduate study in archaeology. Archaeology departments are typically part of anthropology departments; few separate archaeology departments exist in U.S. colleges and universities. As a student of archaeology, you'll follow a program that involves many disciplines, including art, architecture, classics, and history.

Some colleges and universities offer classes, concentrations, or programs in underwater archaeology. One such program is found at Texas A&M University, which offers a master's degree and doctorate in underwater archaeology. Visit the program's Web site, http://nautarch.tamu.edu, for more information. Other schools that offer course work or programs in underwater archaeology include East Carolina University, Florida State University, Indiana University, and the University of West Florida.

Certification or Licensing
The Register of Professional Archaeologists offers voluntary registration to archaeologists who agree to "abide by an explicit code of conduct and standards of research performance; who hold a graduate degree in archaeology, anthropology, art history, classics, history, or another germane discipline; and who have substantial practical experience."

PADI offers voluntary certification to divers. Contact the organization for more information.

Other Requirements
Successful underwater archaeologists are able to work well as part of a team and on their own. They must be excellent researchers and have curious personalities. Strong communication skills are needed

because underwater archaeologists must interact with other members of their team, prepare reports, and write requests for funding.

Underwater archaeologists also need excellent diving skills. They should be mechanically inclined, able to operate and maintain a wide variety of equipment, and have an understanding of the physical and biological elements—especially as they relate to the preservation of artifacts.

Physical requirements for the career include overall good health, at least normal physical strength, sound respiratory functions, normal or better eyesight, and good hand-eye coordination and manual dexterity.

EXPLORING

You can learn about underwater archaeology and archaeology in general by visiting Web sites, reading books and magazines, watching television shows and movies about archaeologists, and participating in an information interview with an underwater archaeologist.

Become proficient in scuba diving and outdoor swimming and diving. The experience of learning to feel at home in water and underwater not only can help you pass entry tests for formal training in diving but also can allow you to find out if you really are suited for a career as an underwater archaeologist.

The Institute of Nautical Archaeology provides a wealth of resources for aspiring underwater archaeologists. At its Web site, you can read sample copies of *The Institute of Nautical Archaeology Quarterly,* read about institute expeditions and founders, view photos of underwater archaeology, read about membership benefits for college students, and find links to other nautical archaeology resources.

EMPLOYERS

Many underwater archaeologists are employed by colleges and universities. They also work for museums, government agencies (such as the National Park Service and state historic preservation offices), and in the private sector.

STARTING OUT

Underwater archaeologists can gain experience in the field by working as research assistants or teaching fellows while in graduate school. This experience makes them more appealing job candidates.

Graduate school professors and college career services are great sources of job leads. Additionally, some professional archaeology associations offer job listings at their Web sites.

ADVANCEMENT

Archaeology is a relatively small field, and the field of underwater archaeology is even smaller. This makes it a challenge at times to advance. Archaeologists employed by museums can advance by receiving pay raises, increased responsibilities, or by being promoted to the position of director or curator (although additional education is required for these jobs). Most archaeology teachers start out as instructors and then proceed up the career ladder to assistant professor, associate professor, and full professor positions. They can also become department heads or seek out other administrative positions at their institution. Archaeologists also advance by becoming experts in their field of study and writing books and articles about their specialty.

EARNINGS

The U.S. Department of Labor (DOL) does not provide specific salary information for underwater archaeologists. Median annual earnings for all archaeologists were $53,460 in 2009, according to the DOL. Salaries ranged from less than $31,530 to $87,890 or more.

Many archaeologists work in academia. According to the DOL, college and university archaeology professors earned between $41,270 and $119,070 in 2009, depending on the type of institution. Median annual earnings were $69,520.

Benefits for full-time workers include paid vacation, health, disability, life insurance, and retirement or pension plans.

WORK ENVIRONMENT

Underwater archaeologists who are employed in academia typically work in comfortable classrooms and offices. Although they may teach only two to three courses a semester, they have to spend considerable time preparing for class, meeting with students, conducting research, and attending to department business. Those working in the field typically live for extended periods of time on research vessels or camps on the shores of lakes, rivers, oceans, or other bodies of water where they are conducting research. Living conditions may be primitive. Archaeologists must work in all types of weather conditions, ranging from extreme heat or cold, to rain, to snow, to windy conditions. Conditions on large bodies of water can be dangerous when a sudden storm occurs.

Underwater archaeologists must be confident of their own ability to cope with the uncertainties and risks of diving. They must be in excellent physical condition in order to endure the challenges of diving and underwater research.

OUTLOOK

Employment for archaeologists is expected to grow much faster than the average for all careers through 2018, according to the U.S. Department of Labor. The employment outlook for underwater archaeologists is also expected to be good. Underwater archaeologists have excavated more than 100 sunken vessels, and technological innovations have allowed them to conduct fieldwork in many areas where it was impossible to work in the past.

It is important to remember that the number of people who specialize in underwater archaeology is small. This makes it difficult to land a job in the field since turnover is low. Many underwater archaeologists work in college and university settings. Opportunities for postsecondary educators are expected to be good through 2018, but it may be difficult for teachers to obtain tenure-track positions.

FOR MORE INFORMATION

The following organization offers valuable information about anthropological careers and student associations:
American Anthropological Association
Archaeology Division
2200 Wilson Boulevard, Suite 600
Arlington, VA 22201-3357
Tel: 703-528-1902
http://www.aaanet.org/sections/ad

For information about the field, contact
Historical Diving Society USA
PO Box 2837
Santa Maria, CA 93457-2837
Tel: 805-934-1660
E-mail: info@hds.org
http://www.hds.org

For information on underwater archaeology, contact
Institute of Nautical Archaeology
PO Drawer HG
College Station, TX 77841-5137
Tel: 979-845-6694
http://inadiscover.com

For information on state archaeologists and archaeology museums and resources, contact
National Association of State Archaeologists
http://www.uiowa.edu/~osa/nasa

For information on diving instruction and certification, contact
PADI
30151 Tomas Street
Rancho Santa Margarita, CA 92688-2125
Tel: 800-729-7234
http://www.padi.com

For information on professional registration, contact
Register of Professional Archaeologists
5024-R Campbell Boulevard
Baltimore, MD 21236-5943
Tel: 410-933-3486
E-mail: info@rpanet.org
http://www.rpanet.org

For information on archaeological careers and job listings, contact
Society for American Archaeology
900 Second Street, NE, Suite 12
Washington, DC 20002-3560
Tel: 202-789-8200
E-mail: headquarters@saa.org
http://www.saa.org

The SAS is an association for "those interested in advancing our knowledge of the past through a wide range of techniques deriving from the fields of physics, chemistry, and the natural sciences." Visit its Web site for more information.
Society for Archaeological Sciences (SAS)
http://www.socarchsci.org

For career information, contact
Society for Historical Archaeology
9707 Key West Avenue, Suite 100
Rockville, MD 20850-3992
Tel: 301-990-2454
E-mail: hq@sha.org
http://www.sha.org
http://www.sha.org/EHA/splash.cfm

For an overview of what it is like to be an archaeologist written by an associate professor of anthropology, visit
Frequently Asked Questions About a Career in Archaeology in the U.S.
http://www.museum.state.il.us/ismdepts/anthro/dlcfaq.html

Writers and Editors

School Subjects
English
History
Journalism

Personal Skills
Communication/ideas
Helping/teaching
Technical/scientific

Work Environment
Indoors and outdoors
One location with some
travel

Minimum Education Level
Bachelor's degree

Salary Range
$28,070 to $53,900 to
$105,710+ (writers)
$28,430 to $50,800 to
$97,360+ (editors)

Certification or Licensing
None available

Outlook
About as fast as the average

DOT
131, 132

GOE
01.02.01

NOC
5121, 5122

O*NET-SOC
27-3041.00, 27-3043.00

OVERVIEW

Writers and *editors* express, edit, promote, and interpret ideas and facts in written and electronic form. *Archaeology writers* write about archaeology and related topics for books, magazines, trade journals, newspapers, technical studies and reports, association and company newsletters, and radio and television broadcasts.

Archaeology editors perform a wide range of functions, but their primary responsibility is to ensure that text provided by archaeology writers is suitable in content, format, and style for the intended audiences. Readers are an editor's first priority.

HISTORY

The skill of writing has existed for thousands of years. Papyrus fragments with writing by ancient Egyptians date from about 3000 B.C., and archaeological findings show that the Chinese had developed books by about 1300 B.C. A number of technical obstacles had to be overcome before printing and the profession of writing evolved. Books of the Middle Ages were copied by hand on parchment. The ornate style that marked these books helped ensure their rarity. Also, few people were able to read. Religious fervor prohibited the reproduction of secular literature.

The development of the printing press by Johannes Gutenberg in the middle of the 15th century and the liberalism of the Protestant Reformation, which helped encourage a wider range of publications, greater literacy, and the creation of a number of works of literary merit, helped develop the publishing industry. The first authors worked directly with printers.

The modern publishing age began in the 18th century. Printing became mechanized, and the novel, magazine, and newspaper developed. The first newspaper in the American colonies appeared in the early 18th century, but it was Benjamin Franklin who, as editor and writer, made the *Pennsylvania Gazette* one of the most influential in setting a high standard for his fellow American journalists. Franklin also published the first magazine in the colonies, *The American Magazine,* in 1741.

Advances in the printing trades, photoengraving, retailing, and the availability of capital produced a boom in newspapers and magazines in the 19th century. Further mechanization in the printing field, such as the use of the Linotype machine, high-speed rotary presses, and special color reproduction processes, set the stage for still further growth in the book, newspaper, and magazine industry.

The history of book editing is tied closely to the history of the book and bookmaking and the history of the printing process. In the early days of publishing, authors worked directly with the printer, and the printer was often the publisher and seller of the author's work. Eventually, however, booksellers began to work directly with the authors and eventually took over the role of publisher. The publisher then became the middleman between author and printer.

The publisher worked closely with the author and sometimes acted as the editor; the word *editor,* in fact, derives from the Latin word *edere* or *editum* and means supervising or directing the preparation of text. Eventually, specialists were hired to perform the editing function. These editors, who were also called advisers or literary advisors in the 19th century, became an integral part of the publishing business.

Archaeology writers and editors have existed as long as archaeological excavations have been conducted. In the early years of archaeological discovery, archaeologists typically wrote articles and books about their findings. Later, skilled writers with a fascination for anthropology and archaeology also began writing about the field for both professional and general audiences. Some of the oldest continuously published periodicals about archaeology in the United States include the *American Journal of Archaeology* (founded in 1885) and *Archaeology* (founded in 1948). *National Geographic,* a magazine that covers a diverse range of issues in history, culture, and the natural world (including those in anthropology and archaeology), was founded in 1888.

In addition to the print media, the broadcasting industry has contributed to the development of the professional writer. Film, radio, and television are sources of entertainment, information, and education that provide employment for thousands of writers. Archaeology writers have written scripts and served as technical advisers for archaeology-oriented documentaries, films, and radio programs.

THE JOB

Writers work in the field of communications. Those who specialize in archaeology focus on creating works of nonfiction or fiction about archaeology and related topics. They produce a wide variety of materials: books; magazine, trade journal, and newspaper articles; technical reports; association newsletters and other publications; scripts for motion picture productions; and scripts for radio and television broadcast. Writers develop ideas and write for all media.

Good writers gather as much information as possible about a subject (for example, the discovery of the ruins of an ancient Zulu village, human sacrifice in the Cahokian mound culture, or a new scientific technique that helps archaeologists more accurately date artifacts) and then carefully check the accuracy of their sources. Usually, this involves extensive library research, interviews with archaeologists and scientists, or long hours of observation and personal experience. Writers keep notes from which they prepare an outline. They often rewrite sections of the material, always searching for the best way to express an idea or opinion. A manuscript may be reviewed, corrected, and revised many times before a final copy is ready.

Writers can be employed either as in-house staff or as freelancers. Freelancers must provide their own office space and equipment such as computers and fax machines. Freelance writers also are responsible for keeping tax records, sending out invoices, negotiating contracts, and providing their own health insurance.

Editors work for many kinds of publishers, companies, and other organizations. Editors' titles vary widely, not only from one area of publishing to another but also within each area. *Book editors* prepare text for publication in print or online. An archaeology editor may edit an archaeology textbook that is geared toward college students, a general interest book about the field such as *Archaeology For Dummies,* a work of fiction that features archaeology as part of its plot line, or a scholarly title that is geared toward archaeology professionals. In small publishing houses, the same editor may guide the material through all the stages of the publishing process. In larger publishing houses, editors tend to be more specialized, being involved in only a part of the publishing process.

Magazines About Archaeology

American Archaeology
http://www.americanarchaeology.com/aamagazine.html

American Journal of Archaeology
http://www.ajaonline.org

Archaeology
http://www.archaeology.org

Archaeology Magazine
http://inadiscover.com/archaeology_resources/archaeology_
  magazine

Biblical Archaeology Review
http://www.bib-arch.org

The Institute of Nautical Archaeology Quarterly
http://inadiscover.com/ina_quarterly

Journal of Field Archaeology
http://www.maney.co.uk/index.php/journals/jfa/

National Geographic
http://www.nationalgeographic.com
http://news.nationalgeographic.com/news/archaeology.html

Preservation
http://www.preservationnation.org/magazine

Acquisitions editors are the editors who find new writers and sign on new projects. They are responsible for finding new ideas for books that will sell well and for finding writers who can create the books.

Production editors are responsible for taking the manuscript written by an author and polishing the work into a finished book. They correct grammar, spelling, and style, and check all the facts. They make sure the book reads well and suggest changes to the author if it does not. The production editor may be responsible for getting the cover designed and the art put into a book. Because the work is so demanding, production editors usually work on only one or two books at a time.

Copy editors assist the production editor in polishing the author's writing. Copy editors review each page and make all the changes required to give the book a good writing style. *Line editors* review the text to make sure specific style rules are obeyed. They make sure the same spelling is used for words where more than one spelling is correct (for example, grey and gray).

Fact checkers and *proofreaders* read the manuscript to make sure everything is spelled correctly and that all the facts in the text have been checked.

The basic functions performed by *magazine and newspaper editors* are much like those performed by book editors, but a significant amount of the writing that appears in magazines and newspapers, or periodicals, is done by staff writers. Archaeology editors who work for a magazine may edit scholarly articles about topics and archaeology techniques that may be of interest only to practitioners and educators or general interest articles that are geared toward the average person without an educational background in archaeology. Like book houses, periodicals use copy editors, researchers, and fact checkers, but at small periodicals, one or a few editors may be responsible for tasks that would be performed by many people at a larger publication.

REQUIREMENTS

High School

If you are interested in becoming a writer or an editor, take English, literature, foreign languages, general science, social studies, computer science, and typing classes while in high school. The ability to type is almost a requisite for all positions in the communications field, as is familiarity with computers.

Editors and writers must be expert communicators, so you should excel in English if you wish to work in these careers. You must learn to write extremely well, since you will be correcting and even rewriting the work of others. If they are offered at your school, take elective classes in writing or editing, such as journalism and business communications.

Don't forget, however, that a successful writer or editor must have a wide range of knowledge. Don't hesitate to explore areas that you find interesting. Do everything you can to satisfy your intellectual curiosity. As far as most writers and editors are concerned, there is no useless information.

If you know that you want to write or edit articles about archaeology, you should take as many classes in history, anthropology, and archaeology as possible in order to increase your knowledge about these fields. Participating in an archaeological dig or visiting archaeology museums will also help you expand your knowledge.

Postsecondary Training

Most writing and editing jobs require a college education. Many employers prefer that you have a broad liberal arts background or majors in English, literature, history, philosophy, or one of the social sciences. Other employers desire communications or journalism training in college. Occasionally a master's degree in a specialized writing or editing field may be required. Most schools offer courses in journalism and some have more specialized courses in book publishing, publication management, and newspaper and magazine writing.

In addition to formal course work, most employers look for practical writing and editing experience. If you have served on high school or college newspapers, yearbooks, or literary magazines, you will make a better candidate, as well as if you have worked for small community newspapers or radio stations, even in an unpaid position. Many book publishers, magazines, newspapers, and radio and television stations have summer internship programs that provide valuable training if you want to learn about the publishing and broadcasting businesses. Interns do many simple tasks, such as running errands and answering phones, but some may be asked to perform research, conduct interviews, or even write or edit some minor pieces.

Writers or editors who specialize in archaeology may need degrees, concentrated course work, or experience in archaeology, anthropology, history, historic preservation, or a related field. Some archaeology writers and editors do not have an educational background in the field, but develop their expertise after years of experience at an archaeology-related publication or publisher.

Other Requirements

Writers and editors should be creative and able to express ideas clearly, have a broad general knowledge, be skilled in research techniques, and be computer literate. Other assets include curiosity, persistence, initiative, resourcefulness, and an accurate memory.

You must be detail oriented to succeed as a writer or an editor. You must also be patient, since you may have to spend hours synthesizing information into the written word or turning a few pages of near-gibberish into powerful, elegant English. If you are the kind of person who can't sit still, you probably will not succeed in these careers. To be a good writer or editor, you must be a self-starter who is not afraid to make decisions. You must be good not only at identifying problems but also at solving them, so you must be creative.

EXPLORING

As a high school or college student, you can test your interest and aptitude in the fields of writing and editing by working as a reporter or writer on school newspapers, yearbooks, and literary magazines. If you cannot work for the school paper, try to land a part-time job on a local newspaper or newsletter. If that doesn't work, you might want to publish your own newsletter. There is nothing like trying to put together a small publication to help you understand how publishing works. You may try combining another interest with your interest in writing or editing. For example, if you are interested in archaeology, you might want to start a blog or a newsletter that deals with archaeology or history. Use your imagination.

Information on writing and editing as a career may also be obtained by visiting local newspapers or publishers and interviewing some of the people who work there. Career conferences and other guidance programs frequently include speakers on the entire field of communications from local or national organizations.

If you are interested in working as an archaeology writer or editor, there are many ways to learn about the field. Read books about archaeology. Visit Web sites about archaeology. Visit archaeology museums. Participate in an archaeological dig or a college archaeology program for high school students during your summer vacation. Write about your experiences in a blog or in your journal. Contact writers and editors at archaeology magazines to see if they will participate in an information interview about their careers. Start an archaeology club at your school. You also might consider subscribing to archaeology-related publications such as *American Archaeology* (http://www.americanarchaeology.com/aamagazine.html), *American Journal of Archaeology* (http://www.ajaonline.org), and *Archaeology* (http://www.archaeology.org). Visit these publications' Web sites to read sample articles and writers' guidelines. *Archaeology* magazine offers a detailed summary of its guidelines for writers at http://www.archaeology.org/write/guidelines.html.

Brian Fagan is one of the most popular mainstream archaeology writers in the world. Visit http://www.brianfagan.com to learn more about his career, find answers to frequently asked questions about a career as a writer, and read excerpts from his books.

EMPLOYERS

About 30 percent of salaried writers and 51 percent of editors work for newspapers, magazines, and book publishers, according to the *Occupational Outlook Handbook*. Only a small percentage specialize in the field of archaeology. Writers and editors are also employed by advertising agencies, in radio and television broadcasting, public relations firms, Internet sites, and for journals and newsletters published by business and nonprofit organizations, such as professional associations, labor unions, and religious organizations. Other employers are government agencies and film production companies.

STARTING OUT

A fair amount of experience is required to gain a high-level position in the writing field. Most writers start out in entry-level positions. These jobs may be listed with college career services offices, or they may be obtained by applying directly to the employment departments of companies. Graduates who previously had internships with these companies often have the advantage of knowing someone who can give them a personal recommendation. Want ads in newspapers and trade journals are another source for jobs. Because of the competition for positions, however, few vacancies are listed with public or private employment agencies.

Employers in the communications field usually are interested in samples of your published writing. These are often assembled in an organized portfolio or scrapbook. Stories with bylines that show you have written the work are more impressive and convincing than stories whose source is not identified.

Beginning positions as a junior writer usually involve library research, preparation of rough drafts for part or all of a report, cataloging, and other related writing tasks. These are generally carried on under the supervision of a senior writer.

There is tremendous competition for editorial jobs, so it is important for a beginner who wishes to break into the business to be as well prepared as possible. College students who have gained experience as interns, have worked for publications during summer vacations, or have attended special programs in publishing will be at an advantage. In addition, applicants for any editorial position must be extremely careful when preparing cover letters and resumes. Even a single error in spelling or usage will disqualify an applicant. Applicants for editorial or proofreading positions must also expect to take and pass tests that are designed to determine their language skills.

Many editors enter the field as editorial assistants or proofreaders. Some editorial assistants perform only clerical tasks, whereas others may also proofread or perform basic editorial tasks. Typically, an editorial assistant who performs well will be given the opportunity to take on more and more editorial duties as time passes. Proofreaders have the advantage of being able to look at the work of editors, so they can learn while they do their own work.

Good sources of information about job openings are school career services offices, classified ads in newspapers and trade journals, specialized publications such as *Publishers Weekly* (http://publishersweekly.com), and Internet sites. One way to proceed is to identify local publishers through the Yellow Pages. Many publishers have Web sites that list job openings, and large publishers often have telephone job lines that serve the same purpose.

ADVANCEMENT

Most writers find their first jobs as editorial or production assistants. Advancement may be more rapid in small companies, where beginners learn by doing a little bit of everything and may be given writing tasks immediately. In large firms, duties are usually more compartmentalized. Assistants in entry-level positions are assigned such tasks as research, fact checking, and copywriting, but it generally takes much longer to advance to full-scale writing duties.

Promotion into more responsible positions may come with the assignment of more important articles and stories to write, or it may be the result of moving to another company. Freelance or self-employed writers earn advancement in the form of larger fees as they gain exposure and establish their reputations.

In book publishing houses, employees who start as editorial assistants or proofreaders and show promise generally become copy editors. After gaining skill in that position, they may be given a wider range of duties while retaining the same title. The next step may be a position as a *senior copy editor,* which involves overseeing the work of junior copy editors, or as a project editor. The *project editor* performs a wide variety of tasks, including copyediting, coordinating the work of in-house and freelance copy editors, and managing the schedule of a particular project. From this position, an editor may move up to become *first assistant editor, then managing editor,* then *editor in chief.* These positions involve more management and decision making than is usually found in the positions described previously. The editor in chief works with the publisher to ensure that a suitable editorial policy is being followed, while the managing editor is responsible for all aspects of the editorial department. The assistant editor provides support to the managing editor.

Newspaper editors generally begin working on the copy desk, where they progress from less significant stories and projects to major news and feature stories. A common route to advancement is for copy editors to be promoted to a particular department, where they may move up the ranks to management positions. An editor who has achieved success in a department may become a *city editor,* who is responsible for news, or a managing editor, who runs the entire editorial operation of a newspaper.

The advancement path for magazine editors is similar to that of book editors. After they become copy editors, they work their way up to become senior editors, managing editors, and editors in chief. In many cases, magazine editors advance by moving from a position on one magazine to the same position with a larger or more prestigious magazine. Such moves often bring significant increases in both pay and status.

EARNINGS

The U.S. Department of Labor does not provide information on salaries for archaeology writers and editors. It does report that all writers earned salaries that ranged from less than $28,070 to more than $105,710 in 2009. Those employed by newspaper, periodical, book, and directory publishers earned annual salaries of $53,050. Median annual earnings for all editors were $50,800 in 2009. Salaries ranged from $28,430 or less to more than $97,360. Those who worked for newspaper, periodical, book, and directory publishers earned annual salaries of $58,580.

In addition to their salaries, many writers and editors earn income from freelance work. Freelance earnings vary widely. Full-time established freelance writers and editors may earn more than $75,000 a year.

Typical benefits may be available for full-time salaried employees including sick leave, vacation pay, and health, life, and disability insurance. Retirement plans may also be available, and some companies may match employees' contributions. Some companies may also offer stock-option plans.

Freelance writers and editors do not receive benefits and are responsible for their own medical, disability, and life insurance. They do not receive vacation pay, and when they aren't working, they aren't generating income. Retirement plans must also be self-funded and self-directed.

WORK ENVIRONMENT

Working conditions vary for writers. Although the workweek usually runs 35 to 40 hours, many writers work overtime. The work is especially hectic on newspapers and at weekly magazines. Writers often work nights and weekends to meet deadlines or to cover a late-developing story.

Most writers work independently, but they often must cooperate with artists, photographers, art directors, rewriters, and advertising people who may have widely differing ideas of how the materials should be prepared and presented.

Physical surroundings range from comfortable private offices to noisy, crowded newsrooms filled with other workers typing and talking on the telephone. Some archaeology writers must confine their research to the library or telephone interviews, but others may travel to other cities or countries or to local sites, such as conservation laboratories, museums, historical societies, and archaeological sites. Conditions at archaeological sites vary greatly. For example, a writer doing a story on recent discoveries in the Valley of the Kings in Egypt may encounter extreme heat and dusty conditions, while one conducting research on ancient burial mounds in Norway may experience extremely cold conditions. Some writers with training in scuba diving may even shadow an underwater archaeologist as he or she explores ancient shipwrecks deep beneath the ocean surface. While conducting research, writers may have to live in primitive conditions, and they will frequently interact with a wide range of cultures.

The work is arduous, but writers are seldom bored. Each day brings new and interesting problems. The most difficult element is the continual pressure of deadlines. People who are the most content as writers enjoy and work well with deadline pressure.

The environments in which editors work vary widely. For the most part, publishers of all kinds realize that a quiet atmosphere is conducive to work that requires tremendous concentration. It takes an unusual ability to focus to edit in a noisy place. Most editors work in private offices or cubicles. Book editors often work in quieter surroundings than do newspaper editors, who sometimes work in rather loud and hectic situations.

Even in relatively quiet surroundings, however, editors often have many distractions. A project editor who is trying to do some copyediting or review the editing of others may, for example, have to deal with phone calls from authors, questions from junior editors, meetings with members of the editorial and production staff, and questions from freelancers, among many other distractions. In many cases, editors have computers that are exclusively for their own use, but in others, editors must share computers that are located in a common area.

Deadlines are an important issue for virtually all editors. Newspaper and magazine editors work in a much more pressurized atmosphere than book editors because they face daily or weekly deadlines, whereas book production usually takes place over several months.

OUTLOOK

The employment of writers and editors is expected to grow about as fast as the average for all occupations through 2018, according to the *Occupational Outlook Handbook*. There will be increasing job opportunities for writers and editors in Internet publishing as online publishing and services continue to grow. While there are a wide variety of openings for general writers and editors, employment openings for writers and editors who specialize in archaeology are few and far between. Only a few magazines specialize in archaeology. Many books are published about archaeology, but their total number comprises a small percentage of all the books that are published.

Individuals entering this field should realize that the competition for jobs is extremely keen. Students just out of college, especially, may have difficulty finding employment. Of the thousands who graduate each year with degrees in English, journalism, communications, and the liberal arts, intending to establish a career as writer or editor, many turn to other occupations when they find that applicants far outnumber the job openings available. College students would do well to keep this in mind and prepare for an alternate career in the event they are unable to obtain a position as writer or editor.

Writers and editors with degrees in archaeology, anthropology, history, and related fields, as well as work experience in these areas, will have the best employment prospects.

FOR MORE INFORMATION

The following organization is an excellent source of information about careers in copyediting. ACES organizes educational seminars and maintains lists of internships.
American Copy Editors Society (ACES)
http://www.copydesk.org

The AAP is an organization of book publishers. Its extensive Web site is a good place to begin learning about the book business.
Association of American Publishers (AAP)
71 Fifth Avenue, 2nd Floor
New York, NY 10003-3004
Tel: 212-255-0200
http://www.publishers.org

The fund provides information about internships and about the newspaper business in general.
Dow Jones News Fund
PO Box 300
Princeton, NJ 08543-0300
Tel: 609-452-2820
E-mail: djnf@dowjones.com
http://www.newsfund.org

The EFA is an organization for freelance editors. Members receive a newsletter and a free listing in their directory.
Editorial Freelancers Association (EFA)
71 West 23rd Street, 4th Floor
New York, NY 10010-4102
Tel: 212-929-5400
E-mail: office@the-efa.org
http://www.the-efa.org

The MPA is a good source of information about internships.
Magazine Publishers of America (MPA)
810 Seventh Avenue, 24th Floor
New York, NY 10019-5873
Tel: 212-872-3700
E-mail: mpa@magazine.org
http://www.magazine.org

Information on writing and editing careers in the field of archaeology is available from
National Association of Science Writers
PO Box 7905
Berkeley, CA 94707-0905
Tel: 510-647-9500
http://www.nasw.org

This organization offers student memberships for those interested in opinion writing.
National Conference of Editorial Writers
3899 North Front Street
Harrisburg, PA 17110-1583
Tel: 717-703-3015
E-mail: ncew@pa-news.org
http://www.ncew.org

═══ **INTERVIEW** ═══

Michael Bawaya is the editor of American Archaeology, *a quarterly publication of* The Archaeological Conservancy. *He discussed his career with the editors of* Careers in Focus: Archaeology.

Q. Can you tell us a little about yourself and *American Archaeology*?

A. I've been editor of *American Archaeology* for 10 years. Prior to that I edited business, travel, and performing arts publications. I've also written for a number of national and regional publications. I have a bachelor's degree in journalism and had no experience in archaeology prior to being hired.

American Archaeology is a national magazine with a circulation of around 25,000. It's written for a general audience. The magazine, which is 12 years old, is published by The Archaeological Conservancy, a nonprofit organization that preserves archaeological sites.

Q. Can you please describe a day in your life on the job? What are your typical work responsibilities?

A. My major responsibilities include setting a production schedule, and developing and editing stories for the magazine. If someone suggests an idea for a story, I have to research it to make sure it has the potential to be an article that's suitable for *American Archaeology*. Assuming it does, I then hire a writer to do it. This requires giving the writer some basic information about the story, including major sources, and some guidance as to how to approach the topic. I also coordinate with my art director so she can obtain images that complement the piece. I then edit the stories. In the worst cases, I have to rewrite them.

Q. What are the most important personal and professional qualities for editors?

A. Editors have to be creative, organized, and good communicators. They have to be able to see the big picture, work under deadline pressure, deal with several different projects simultaneously, and solve problems. The work can be stressful, and I think it's important to handle the challenges, and the people I deal with, with calm and courtesy.

Q. What are some of the pros and cons of your job?

A. Pros: Traveling to archaeological sites, some of which are in faraway places, to write about the work being done there. Collaborating with some of the talented people who contribute to the publication.

Cons: Making sure everybody more or less meets their deadlines. Criticizing, and sometimes rejecting, the work of contributors.

Q. What have been some of your most rewarding experiences in your career and why?

A. Seeing a mere idea blossom into a well-written article, complete with compelling images, is gratifying. Receiving compliments from readers about a particular article, or the magazine in general, is also nice. Writing articles is also fun, as is learning about archaeology.

Index

Entries and page numbers in **bold** indicate major treatment of a topic.

A